The Berezina

The Armies of 1812

S. Henry Dwan

SHD
PRESS

Cover painting
Polish painter January Suchodolski's 'The French Army crossing the Berezina'. The sheer scope of the crossing is dramatically captured in fine detail in this picture. Napoleon and his staff are visible near the bridge to the right (which remains intact) whilst the other bridge has broken. Desperate soldiers are swimming the frozen river as the few remaining cavalry and transport vehicles make their way forward. The Guard infantry can be seen marching up in the centre of the picture.

BOOK EIGHTEEN IN THE ORDERS OF BATTLE SERIES

Other titles in this series:

Contents

Introduction

By June 1812 France and Russia were at war again after a peace that had lasted just five years. Once a French ally, Russia had pulled away from the Napoleonic yolk when her interests were no longer upheld by what appeared to be a one sided relationship. Napoleon sought to bring on an early defeat of the Russian armies in the west, which he hoped would bring the Czar back into the fold. His instrument to achieve this was the largest army he would ever command. Some 612,000 men were assembled and almost three quarters of them marched into Russia in June 1812.

Advancing as far as Moscow, Napoleon's central army group of 250,000 shrunk at an alarming rate throughout the summer advance. The 100,000 who got this far then delayed their stay in the city for five weeks, before beginning a retreat to a more sustainable position that could be supplied and reinforced. Intending to follow a more fertile southern route westwards, instead of the ravaged invasion route, *La Grande Armée* was checked and driven back north to the very road they wished to avoid. The first snow fell on 4th November and with few supplies and fodder available along the Smolensk road, the army was soon suffering from starvation and cold.

As men and horses fell out of the column every day, the Russians under Kutuzov were content to follow and let the cold and the cossacks whittle their enemy down. In the meantime, more Russian forces who had remained in the north and south during the summer, were directed to intercept the broken invaders as they tried to make their way out of Russia. A number of battles were fought with the major one taking place at the Berezina river crossing at the end of November. Having received reinforcements, Napoleon had almost 50,000 combatants (there were also 40,000 stragglers) but he was facing odds approaching 2:1. Despite this, the crossing of the river was skilfully managed and victory was achieved but at a high cost.

The retreat would continue until a few thousand of those who marched on Moscow returned, and overall about half a million men were lost in this disastrous campaign. Sensing the French empire was on its knees, the major powers made an alliance and a new war began in 1813 that would last until Napoleon was finally defeated in April 1814.

This eighteenth volume in the Orders of Battle series covers the French-allied and Russian armies present at the battle of the Berezina and some of the actions immediately preceding it. As with previous volumes in the series, an outline to the armies and a brief synopsis of the battle and earlier engagements is included along with a detailed representation of the corps, regiments, squadrons and artillery batteries present. Use has been made of numerous available orders of battle to ensure accuracy by cross referencing and drawing the best elements of each to produce the most complete record. Extensive research has also been made of the uniforms worn and the flag standards carried by the individual regiments to give an accurate visual interpretation of the way each unit would have actually appeared at the battles rather than its prescribed 'parade uniform'. A scale of 1:10 has been used to help visualise a precise image of the actual size of each unit. Finally, the text describing the units, their strength and commanders completes what is hoped to be the most complete and understandable record available.

La Grande Armée of 1812

The immense multi-national force of 612,000 men that crossed that crossed the Nieman five months earlier was by November, a sad shadow of itself. Natural wastage had begun immediately the advance into Russia began. The central core of about 450,000 men had been startlingly reduced as the advance carried them eastwards, ever deeper into the country as Napoleon sought in vain to bring the Russians to a major decisive battle. Horses had died in droves during the advance, in part due to sudden changes in weather and the consumption of un-ripened rye. Cavalry regiments that had begun the campaign at brigade size, had by the time they fought at Borodino, been reduced by more than two thirds. Draught animals too had been lost at irreplaceable rates, only exacerbating an overstretched supply system.

Of the quarter million that made up the central army group marching via Vitebsk, Minsk and Smolensk, just over half were actually present at Borodino on 7th September. A deserted and burning Moscow had been taken a week later, but with his position becoming daily more and more untenable, Napoleon had withdrawn from the city with around 108,000 survivors on 19th October – having spent five weeks in occupation whilst awaiting peace proposals from the Czar that never came. Attempting at first to withdraw along a more southern route towards Smolensk in order to avoid land already stripped bare of supplies and forage during the advance, Napoleon was defeated by a rejuvenated and rested Russian army under Kutuzov five days later at Maloyaroslavets. Forced to withdraw north to follow the same route back along the Smolensk road, *La Grande Armée's* fate had been sealed.

The weather had been deceptively mild for the time of year but after the first snow fell on 4th November the dreaded Russian winter settled in and by 9th November the temperature dropped to -9c then dropped further to -21c five days later. As roads became covered with ice, horses were unable to keep their footing and broken legs were commonplace (only the Poles had taken the precaution to rough-shod their draught and cavalry animals) and more horses were lost and guns abandoned.

Above: French infantry at the battle of the Berezina. In temperatures of -20c troops were utilizing whatever was available to help them stay warm.

With cold, starvation and hypothermia eating away at an army unprepared for a harsh winter and without suitable clothing for the severe conditions, discipline broke down quickly and the soldiers began falling behind or simply giving up and leaving their regiments. By the time the major obstacle of the river Berezina was reached towards the end of November and with temperatures still around -20c, less that 50,000 combatants remained – which included reinforcements provided by the supporting corps of Oudinot and Victor – along with 40,000 stragglers. The army could still field around 250 guns but many of the *corps d'armée* that had fought at Borodino, had by Berezina been reduced to such an extent that divisions were now at battalion strength.

The cavalry that had quartered in Moscow had all but vanished or its dismounted personnel had been incorporated into the infantry units – apart from the Imperial Guard regiments who could still count on around 2,000 mounted men. Most of the operational cavalry would be provided by the regiments that had recently arrived as reinforcements. Many of the officers from General down, who still possessed a horse and who had no troops left to command, had been called together on 23rd November and formed into a 600 man unit known as 'the sacred squadron' under the command of *Général de division* Grouchy. They were under orders to provide imperial escort duty and remain close to Napoleon and his staff at all times.

Above; French Imperial Guard cavalry in November 1812 (1) The Empress' Dragoons and (2) 1st (Polish) Chevaux-leger Lancers. The Guard was still able to field about 2,000 mounted troopers at this time.

The crossing of the river itself would prove a monumental task since the army had abandoned the pontoon train in the belief that the Berezina would remain frozen and allow a crossing on foot. An unseasonal thaw though, had melted much of the ice and to compound this, the Russians had destroyed the permanent bridge at Studienka. The sappers and *pontonniers* assigned to the various *corps d'armée* were grouped together under *Général de division* Eblé. Eblé had also managed to preserve several field forges to aid in the construction of two 300 foot bridges that would carry vehicles and troops across the river. Many of the men employed in the building of the bridges would however, die from working chest deep in the frozen water.

With much of the force that had left Moscow so badly reduced, most of the troops who would be involved in the battle were from the allied contingents who had been held back in reserve during the advance – most notably the Swiss, Dutch, Poles, Badeners and Bergisch. Whilst the Berezina would be a tactical victory for Napoleon since he was able to extricate the survivors from the designs of the encircling Russian armies, the river crossing only gave brief respite to his army and another 250 mile march in temperatures as low as -37c remained before 10,000 armed and organised survivors with 100,000 stragglers following on, arrived back at the river Nieman on 14th December.

The Russian Armies in 1812

Following the defeat at Borodino, Kutuzov had been careful to preserve his remaining troops and avoided any subsequent confrontation with the French, allowing them to capture Moscow without further resistance. While Napoleon waited in Moscow for five weeks for an answer to his peace proposals that never came, Kutuzov was busy in the location of Podolsk and Tarutino rebuilding his army and providing them with supplies from the fertile south. The Russian 1st and 2nd Western Armies had lost about 45,000 men at Borodino and the withdrawal to Tarutino. But with new conscripts and fresh mounts arriving daily, these loses would soon be replaced. Accused of abandoning Russia's second capital by both his subordinates and by the Czar, the old field-marshal refused to attack until the situation was favourable and the French had begun their inevitable retreat. When that retreat did begin (the day after Murat's 20,000 men were surprised at Winkovo by 90,000 Russians under Bennigsen) Kutuzov followed at a respectful distance along the Smolensk road.

The army of the Danube under the command of Admiral Chichagov had been released in the south since the end of the Russo-Turkish war. This experienced and capable army linked up with the 3rd Western Army and the Army of Finland. Together these troops were given a dual purpose – to prevent field marshal-von Schwarzenberg's Austrians and *Général de division* Reynier's Saxons from offering assistance to the retreating soldiers of *La Grande Armée* whilst manoeuvring to block their escape route. In total these secondary armies would provide about 64,000 men to add to Kutuzov's 65,000 marching from the east. In the freezing temperatures, the Russian troops were only marginally better protected from the elements than the French and many of the new conscripts were lost in the forced marches. They were however, far better provided for and could expect to be fed regularly.

Above: Russian cuirassier during the winter of 1812

Above: Russian infantry during the winter of 1812

Right: French and Russian Commanders in 1812 (1) Maréchal Victor, commander of the 9th Corps (2) Maréchal Oudinot, commander of the 2nd Corps (3) Prince Eugene de Beauharnais, Viceroy of Italy, commander of the 4th Corps (4) Admiral Tchichagov, commander of the Russian Army of the Danube (5) General of Cavalry Wittgenstein, commander of the Russian Right Wing (6) Generalleutnant Steinheil, commander of the Russian Army of Finland.

The Capture of Minsk

17ᵗʰ November 1812
Commanders & Units

French Forces

Commander:
Général de brigade
Bronikowski & staff

Minsk Garrison

Colonel Stanislas
Czapski

1st Battalion, 22nd Lithuanian Infantry Regiment
(700 officers & men)

2nd Battalion, 22nd Lithuanian Infantry Regiment
(700 officers & men)

Major & staff

French Bataillon de Marche (600 officers & men)

Transport & Supply

Company, Lithuanian Equipment Train

Company, Military Equipage Battalion

Medical Service

Ambulance Company

Russian Army of the Danube

Advance Guard

Commander:
Generalmajor Count
Lambert & staff

Colonel & staff

1st Battalion, 10th Jäger Regiment
(400 officers & men)

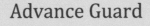

Colonel & staff

1st Battalion, 14th Jäger Regiment
(370 officers & men)

3rd Battalion, 10th Jäger Regiment
(400 officers & men)

3rd Battalion, 14th Jäger Regiment
(370 officers & men)

Artillery

Colonel & staff

11th Horse Battery (8 x 6 pdrs, 4 x 10 pdr Licornes,
216 officers & men)

12th Horse Battery (8 x 6 pdrs, 4 x 10 pdr Licornes,
216 officers & men)

Company, Equipment Train

Ambulance Company

22nd Position (Foot) Battery (8 x 12 pdrs, 4 x 20
pdr unicorns, 233 officers & men)

Company, Equipment Train

Transport, Supply &
Medical Service

Advance Guard

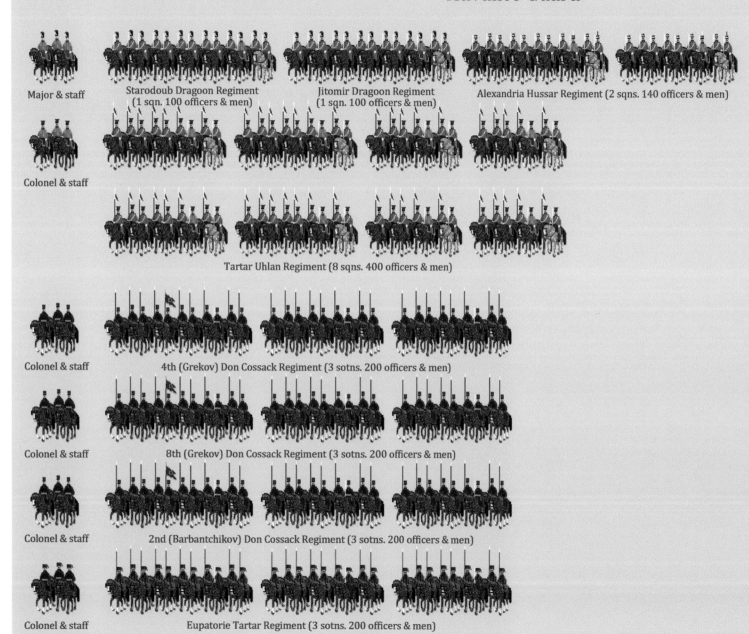

Major & staff

Starodoub Dragoon Regiment
(1 sqn. 100 officers & men)

Jitomir Dragoon Regiment
(1 sqn. 100 officers & men)

Alexandria Hussar Regiment (2 sqns. 140 officers & men)

Colonel & staff

Tartar Uhlan Regiment (8 sqns. 400 officers & men)

Colonel & staff

4th (Grekov) Don Cossack Regiment (3 sotns. 200 officers & men)

Colonel & staff

8th (Grekov) Don Cossack Regiment (3 sotns. 200 officers & men)

Colonel & staff

2nd (Barbantchikov) Don Cossack Regiment (3 sotns. 200 officers & men)

Colonel & staff

Eupatorie Tartar Regiment (3 sotns. 200 officers & men)

The first clash at Borisov

21st November 1812
Commanders & Units

French Forces

17th Division

Commander:
Général de division
Dombrowski & staff

1st Brigade

Général de brigade Zoltowski

Colonel Małachowski

1st Battalion, 1st Polish Infantry Regiment (360 officers & men)

2nd Battalion, 1st Polish Infantry Regiment (360 officers & men)

3rd Battalion, 1st Polish Infantry Regiment (360 officers & men)

Colonel Sierawski

1st Battalion, 6th Polish Infantry Regiment (320 officers & men)

2nd Battalion, 6th Polish Infantry Regiment (320 officers & men)

2nd Brigade

Général de brigade Pakosz

Colonel Siemianowski

1st Battalion, 14th Polish Infantry Regiment (360 officers & men)

2nd Battalion, 14th Polish Infantry Regiment (360 officers & men)

Colonel Hornowski

1st Battalion, 17th Polish Infantry Regiment (320 officers & men)

2nd Battalion, 17th Polish Infantry Regiment (320 officers & men)

Artillery

Major Gugenmus & staff

11th Coy. Polish Foot Artillery Regiment (4 x 6 pdrs, 2 x 24 pdr howitzers, 96 officers & men)

Combined coys. Polish Artillery Train Battalion (85 officers & men)

Transport & Supply

Company, Polish Equipment Train

French Forces

Attached Infantry

Colonel
Lafitte & staff

1st Combined Battalion, 72nd
Infantry Regiment de Ligne
(300 officers & men)

2nd Combined Battalion, 72nd
Infantry Regiment de Ligne
(300 officers & men)

Colonel Schmitza
& staff

The Illyrian Infantry Regiment
(320 officers & men)

Colonel De
Fezensac
& staff

4th Infantry Regiment de
Ligne (220 officers & men)

Colonel
Achard & staff

108th Infantry Regiment de
Ligne (240 officers & men)

Artillery

Combined coys. Artillerie à Pied (6 x 6 pdrs,
2 x 24 pdr howitzers, 92 officers & men)

Combined coys. Artillerie à Cheval (4 x 6 pdrs, 2
x 24 pdr howitzers, 92 officers & men)

Combined coys. Principal Train Battalion (75 officers & men)   Combined coys. Principal Train Battalion (75 officers & men)

Transport, Supply
& Medical Service

Company, Military Equipage
Battalion

Ambulance Company

French Forces

Attached Cavalry

Colonel Piasecki
& staff

2nd Polish Uhlan Regiment (3 sqns. 220 officers & men)

Colonel Zawadzki
& staff

7th Polish Uhlan Regiment (3 sqns. 220 officers & men)

Commander: Général
de division Lefevbre-
Desnouettes & staff

2nd Guard Cavalry Brigade

Général de
brigade Guyot

Chasseurs à Cheval de la Garde (Old Guard) (2 sqns. 450 officers & men)

Chef de Escadron Karmann
& the Squadron de
Mamelukes (Old Guard)
(1 coy. 40 officers & men)

Advance Guard

Commander:
Generalmajor Count
Lambert & staff

Colonel & staff

1st Battalion, 14th Jäger Regiment
(370 officers & men)

2nd Battalion, 14th Jäger Regiment
(370 officers & men)

3rd Battalion, 14th Jäger Regiment
(370 officers & men)

Colonel & staff

1st Battalion, 27th Jäger Regiment
(400 officers & men)

3rd Battalion, 27th Jäger Regiment
(400 officers & men)

Colonel & staff

1st Battalion, 38th Jäger Regiment
(400 officers & men)

3rd Battalion, 38th Jäger Regiment
(400 officers & men)

Colonel & staff

1st Battalion, Vitebsk Infantry Regiment
(400 officers & men)

3rd Battalion, Vitebsk Infantry Regiment
(400 officers & men)

Advance Guard

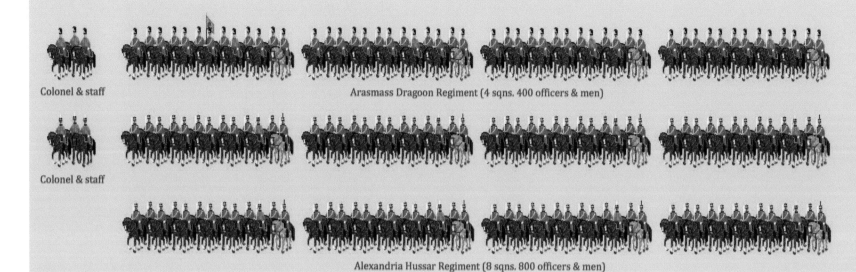

Colonel & staff

Colonel & staff

Arasmass Dragoon Regiment (4 sqns. 400 officers & men)

Alexandria Hussar Regiment (8 sqns. 800 officers & men)

Transport & Supply

Company, Equipment Train

Medical Service

Ambulance Company

Russian Army of the Danube

Advance Guard

Artillery

Colonel & staff

11th Horse Battery (8 x 6 pdrs, 4 x 10 pdr Licornes, 216 officers & men)

12th Horse Battery (8 x 6 pdrs, 4 x 10 pdr Licornes, 216 officers & men)

22nd Position (Foot) Battery (8 x 12 pdrs, 4 x 20 pdr unicorns, 233 officers & men)

Transport & Supply

Company, Equipment Train

Medical Service

Ambulance Company

The clash at Baturi

24th November 1812
Commanders & Units

French Forces

26th Division

Commander:
Général de division
Daendels & staff

Commander:
Général de brigade
Damas & staff

1st (Berg) Brigade

Oberst Genty
& staff

1st Battalion, 1st Berg Infantry Regiment
(480 officers & men)

2nd Battalion, 1st Berg Infantry Regiment
(480 officers & men)

Oberst Forch
& staff

1st Battalion, 4th Berg Infantry Regiment
(480 officers & men)

2nd Battalion, 4th Berg Infantry Regiment
(480 officers & men)

Commander:
Général de brigade
Lingg & staff

2nd (Berg) Brigade

Oberst Hoffmeyer
& staff

1st Battalion, 2nd Berg Infantry Regiment
(480 officers & men)

2nd Battalion, 2nd Berg Infantry Regiment
(480 officers & men)

Oberst Boisdavid
& staff

1st Battalion, 3rd Berg Infantry Regiment
(480 officers & men)

2nd Battalion, 3rd Berg Infantry Regiment
(480 officers & men)

French Forces

26th Division

Commander:
Generalmajor
Hochberg & staff

3rd (Baden) Brigade

Oberst Van
Francken & staff

1st Battalion, 1st (Leib) Infantry Regiment
(480 officers & men)

Oberst Bruckner
& staff

1st Battalion, 3rd (Hochberg) Infantry Regiment
(480 officers & men)

Major & staff

1st (Lingg) Baden Jäger Battalion
(480 officers & men)

2nd Battalion, 1st (Leib) Infantry Regiment
(480 officers & men)

2nd Battalion, 3rd (Hochberg) Infantry Regiment
(480 officers & men)

Artillery

Oberstleutnant
Bogaert & staff

Berg Foot Artillery Battery (6 x 6 pdr cannons,
2 x 24 pdr howitzers, 100 officers & men)

Berg Horse Artillery Battery (4 x 6 pdr cannons,
2 x 24 pdr howitzers, 80 officers & men)

Coy. Berg Artillery Train Battalion (85 officers & men)

Coy. Berg Artillery Train Battalion (65 officers & men)

Baden Foot Artillery Battery (4 x 6 pdr
cannons, 65 officers & men)

Coy. Baden Artillery Train Battalion (55 officers & men)

Baden Horse Artillery Battery (4 x 6 pdr
cannons, 50 officers & men)

Coy. Baden Artillery Train Battalion (45 officers & men)

Transport & Supply

Baden Military Equipage Company

Transport & Supply

Berg Military Equipage Company

Russian Forces – Right Wing

Commander:
Generalmajor
Harpe & staff

Advance Guard

Colonel & staff

1st Battalion, Navaginsk Infantry Regiment
(563 officers & men)

3rd Battalion, Navaginsk Infantry Regiment
(563 officers & men)

Major Sergeev
& staff

1st Battalion, Petrovski Infantry
Regiment (264 officers & men)

3rd Battalion, Petrovski Infantry
Regiment (264 officers & men)

Artillery

Det. 24th Light (Foot) Battery (6 x 6
pdrs, 77 officers & men)

Transport, Supply & Medical Service

Company, Equipment Train

Ambulance Company

Russian Forces – Right Wing

Commander:
Colonel & staff

Grenadier Division (part)

Lt. Colonel & staff

1st Battalion, Combined Grenadiers of 5th Division
(508 officers & men)

2nd Battalion, Combined Grenadiers of 5th Division
(508 officers & men)

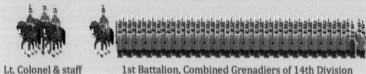 

Lt. Colonel & staff

1st Battalion, Combined Grenadiers of 14th Division
(486 officers & men)

2nd Battalion, Combined Grenadiers of 14th Division
(486 officers & men)

Major & staff

Depot Battalion, Corps Grenadiers
(288 officers & men)

Transport & Supply

Company, Equipment Train

Medical Service

Ambulance Company

Russian Forces – Right Wing

Cavalry

Colonel & staff

1st Platov Don Cossack Regiment (4 sotns. 336 officers & men)

Colonel & staff

Grodno Hussar Regiment (8 sqns. 1,044 officers & men)

Colonel & staff

Combined Dragoon Squadrons (4 sqns. 400 officers & men)

Artillery

23rd Horse Battery (8 x 6 pdrs, 102 officers & men)

The Combat at Staroi-Borisov

27th November 1812
Commanders & Units

French Forces

Commander:
Général de division
Partoneaux & staff

12th Division

Commander:
Général de brigade
Billard & staff

1st Brigade

Chef de bataillon
& staff

4th Battalion 10th Regiment de Légère
(720 officers & men)

Chef de bataillon
& staff

3rd Battalion 44th Regiment de Ligne
(600 officers & men)

4th Battalion 44th Regiment de Ligne
(600 officers & men)

Colonel Sibille
& staff

20th Coy. 5th Artillerie à Pied
(4 x 6 pdrs, 2 x 24 pdr
howitzers, 85 officers & men)

Artillery

1st Coy. 14th Principal Train Battalion
(60 officers & men)

Transport & Supply

Company, Military Equipage Battalion

Medical Service

Ambulance Company
(50 surgeons and men)

French Forces

12th Division

2nd Brigade

Commander: Général
de brigade Blammont
& staff

Colonel Wagner
& staff

1st Battalion 125th (Dutch) Regiment de Ligne
(620 officers & men)

2nd Battalion 125th (Dutch) Regiment de Ligne
(620 officers & men)

3rd Battalion 125th (Dutch) Regiment de Ligne
(620 officers & men)

Colonel Demoulin
& staff

1st Battalion 126th (Dutch) Regiment de Ligne
(640 officers & men)

2nd Battalion 126th (Dutch) Regiment de Ligne
(640 officers & men)

3rd Battalion 126th (Dutch) Regiment de Ligne
(640 officers & men)

4th Battalion 126th (Dutch) Regiment de Ligne
(640 officers & men)

Transport & Supply

Company, Military Equipage Battalion

Medical Service

Ambulance Company
(50 surgeons and men)

French Forces

Commander:
Général de brigade
Camas & staff

12th Division

3rd Brigade

Colonel
Bruneteau de
Saint-Suzanne
& staff

1st Battalion 29th Regiment de Légère
(640 officers & men)

2nd Battalion 29th Regiment de Légère
(640 officers & men)

3rd Battalion 29th Regiment de Légère
(640 officers & men)

4th Battalion 29th Regiment de Légère
(640 officers & men)

Chef de bataillon
& staff

4th Battalion 36th Regiment de Ligne
(640 officers & men)

4th Battalion 51st Regiment de Ligne
(640 officers & men)

Provisional Infantry Regiment

4th Battalion 55th Regiment de Ligne
(640 officers & men)

Attached Cavalry

Oberst & staff

Saxon Prinz Johann Chevauleger Regiment
(4 sqns. 480 officers & men)

Russian Forces

Advance Guard
(from I Corps)

Commander:
Generalmajor
Vlastov & staff

Colonel & staff

1st Battalion, Navaginsk Infantry Regiment
(563 officers & men)

3rd Battalion, Navaginsk Infantry Regiment
(563 officers & men)

Colonel & staff

1st Battalion, 26th Jäger Regiment
(620 officers & men)

3rd Battalion, 26th Jäger Regiment
(620 officers & men)

7th Battalion, St.Petersburg Militia Regiment
(400 officers & men)

Transport & Supply

Company, Equipment Train

Medical Service

Ambulance Company

Russian Forces

Major & staff

Riga Dragoon Regiment (1 sqn. 120 officers & men)

Polish Uhlan Regiment (1 sqn. 120 officers & men)

Advance Guard
(from I Corps)

1 Sotnia, Don Cossacks (1 sotn. 100 officers & men)

Detachment of Kalmucks (60 officers & men)

Artillery

Colonel & staff

9th Light (Foot) Battery (6 x 6 pdrs, 6 x 10 pdr unicorns, 141 officers & men)

27th Position (Foot) Battery (8 x 12 pdrs, 4 x 20 pdr unicorns, 213 officers & men)

Transport & Supply

Medical Service

Company, Equipment Train

Ambulance Company

Right Flank Corps

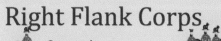

Commander:
Generalleutnant
Steinheil

ADCs to
Generalleutnant
Steinheil

Chief of Staff:
Generalmajor
& staff

Commander:
Generalleutnant
Sazanov & staff

14th Division

Commander:
Generalmajor
& staff

1st Brigade

Colonel & staff

1st Battalion, Toula Infantry Regiment
(578 officers & men)

3rd Battalion, Toula Infantry Regiment
(578 officers & men)

Commander:
Generalmajor
& staff

2nd Brigade

Colonel & staff

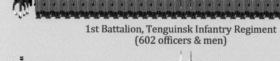

1st Battalion, Tenguinsk Infantry Regiment
(602 officers & men)

3rd Battalion, Tenguinsk Infantry Regiment
(602 officers & men)

Colonel & staff

1st Battalion, Estonia Infantry Regiment
(616 officers & men)

3rd Battalion, Estonia Infantry Regiment
(616 officers & men)

Right Flank Corps

Commander:
Generalmajor
& staff

Cavalry Brigade

Colonel & staff

Finland Dragoon Regiment (4 sqns. 300 officers & men)

Colonel & staff

Mitau Dragoon Regiment (4 sqns. 300 officers & men)

Colonel & staff

Poschilin Cossack Regiment (5 sotns. 300 officers & men)

Transport & Supply

Company, Equipment Train

Medical Service

Ambulance Company

Right Flank Corps

Commander:
Generalamjor
Adadurov & staff

21st Division

Commander:
Colonel Maslov
& staff

1st Brigade

Colonel & staff

1st Battalion, Lithuania Infantry
Regiment (264 officers & men)

3rd Battalion, Lithuania Infantry
Regiment (264 officers & men)

Colonel & staff

1st Battalion, Voronesch Infantry
Regiment (264 officers & men)

2nd Battalion, Voronesch Infantry
Regiment (264 officers & men)

3rd Battalion, Voronesch Infantry
Regiment (264 officers & men)

Colonel & staff

Artillery

6th Position (Foot) Battery (8 x 12 pdrs, 4 x 20
pdr unicorns, 233 officers & men)

9th Light (Foot) Battery (6 x 6 pdrs, 6 x 10 pdr
unicorns, 160 officers & men)

28th Light (Foot) Battery (4 x 6 pdrs,
60 officers & men)

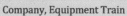

Transport & Supply

Company, Equipment Train

Medical Service

Ambulance Company

Right Flank Corps

21st Division

2nd Brigade

Commander:
Colonel Rosen
& staff

Colonel Sheele
& staff

1st Battalion, Nevaski Infantry
Regiment (264 officers & men)

3rd Battalion, Nevaski Infantry
Regiment (264 officers & men)

 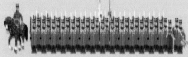 

Major Sergeev
& staff

1st Battalion, Petrovski Infantry
Regiment (264 officers & men)

3rd Battalion, Petrovski Infantry
Regiment (264 officers & men)

Colonel & staff

1st Battalion, St.Petersburg Militia Regiment
(400 officers & men)

2nd Battalion, St.Petersburg Militia Regiment
(400 officers & men)

3rd Battalion, St.Petersburg Militia Regiment
(400 officers & men)

Transport & Supply

Company, Equipment Train

Medical Service

Ambulance Company

Left Flank Corps

Commander:
Generalmajor
Berg & staff

5th Division

Commander:
Generalmajor
& staff

Colonel & staff

1st Battalion, Perm Infantry Regiment
(608 officers & men)

3rd Battalion, Perm Infantry Regiment
(607 officers & men)

Colonel & staff

1st Battalion, Mohilev Infantry Regiment
(618 officers & men)

3rd Battalion, Mohilev Infantry Regiment
(617 officers & men)

Colonel & staff

1st Battalion, Sievsk Infantry Regiment
(618 officers & men)

3rd Battalion, Sievsk Infantry Regiment
(618 officers & men)

Artillery

Colonel & staff

Company, Equipment Train

Transport, Supply & Medical Service

5th Position (Foot) Battery (8 x 12 pdrs, 4 x 20 pdr
unicorns, 213 officers & men)

27th Light (Foot) Battery (6 x 6 pdrs, 6 x 10 pdr
unicorns, 141 officers & men)

Ambulance Company

Left Flank Corps

5th Division

Commander:
Generalmajor
Kulnev & staff

Attached Brigade

Colonel & staff

1st Battalion, Azov Infantry
Regiment (265 officers & men)

3rd Battalion, Azov Infantry
Regiment (265 officers & men)

Lt. Colonel & staff

3rd Battalion, 11th Jäger Regiment
(360 officers & men)

3rd Battalion, 18th Jäger Regiment
(358 officers & men)

3rd Battalion, 36th Jäger Regiment
(420 officers & men)

Combined Jäger
Regiment

Major & staff

Reserve Sqn. Garde Hussar Regiment
(1 sqn.144 officers & men)

Reserve Sqn. Garde Uhlan Regiment
(1 sqn.130 officers & men)

Reserve Sqn. Garde Dragoon Regiment
(1 sqn.130 officers & men)

Colonel & staff

Iamberg Dragoon Regiment (4 sqns. 400 officers & men)

Transport & Supply

Company, Equipment Train

Medical Service

Ambulance Company

The Battle of the Berezina

28-29th November 1812
Commanders & Army Corps

La Grande Armée

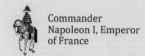

Commander
Napoleon I, Emperor
of France

La Maison Civile

Aides-de-camp to the Emperor

Ordinance Officers

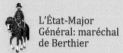

L'État-Major
Général: maréchal
de Berthier

ADCs to
maréchal
de Berthier

Staff of maréchal Berthier

Officers of the Staff

Commander: Général de
division Grouchy & staff

1st Company

2nd Company

The Emperor's Escort

3rd Company

4th Company

L'escadron sacré (4 Coys, 600 Generals, Colonels and other officers still mounted)

Imperial Guard - Vielle Guard

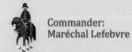
Commander:
Maréchal Lefebvre

ADCs to
Maréchal
Lefebvre

Chief of Staff:
Général de
division & staff

3rd Division of the Guard

Commander:
Général de
division Curial
& staff

1st Brigade

Général de brigade Boyer
& Général de brigade
Baron Gros & staff

1st Battalion, 1st Regiment de Chasseurs à Pied
(460 officers & men)

Major Baron
Rozet & staff

1st Battalion, 2nd Regiment de Chasseurs à Pied
(440 officers & men)

2nd Battalion, 1st Regiment de Chasseurs à Pied
(460 officers & men)

2nd Battalion, 2nd Regiment de Chasseurs à Pied
(440 officers & men)

2nd Brigade

Général de brigade
Michel & Colonel Lored
de Legras & staff

1st Battalion, 1st Regiment de Grenadiers à Pied
(460 officers & men)

Colonel Baron
Harl & staff

1st Battalion, 2nd Regiment de Grenadiers à Pied
(455 officers & men)

Général de
brigade Tindal
& staff

1st Battalion, 3rd (Dutch) Regiment de Grenadiers
à Pied (460 officers & men)

2nd Battalion, 1st Regiment de Grenadiers à Pied
(460 officers & men)

2nd Battalion, 2nd Regiment de Grenadiers à Pied
(455 officers & men)

2nd Battalion, 3rd (Dutch) Regiment de Grenadiers
à Pied (455 officers & men)

Chef de
bataillon
Cotton & staff

1st Coy. (Old) Guard Artillerie à Pied (6 x 12
pdrs, 2 x 5-7" howitzers, 95 officers & men)

2nd Coy. (Young) Guard Artillerie à Pied (6 x 6
pdrs, 2 x 5-7" howitzers, 95 officers & men)

Artillery

Coy. 1st Guard Train Regiment (75 officers & men)

Coy. 1st Guard Train Regiment (75 officers & men)

Imperial Guard - Jeune Guard

Commander:
Maréchal
Mortier

ADCs to
Maréchal
Mortier

Chief of Staff:
Général de
division & staff

Commander:
Général de division
Delaborde & staff

1st Division of the Guard

1st Brigade

Général de brigade
Berthezène & Colonel-
Major Simon Robert

4th Regiment de Tirailleurs
(320 officers & men)

Colonel-
Major baron
Nagle & staff

4th Regiment de Voltigeurs
(320 officers & men)

Colonel-
Major Sicard
& staff

5th Regiment de Voltigeurs
(300 officers & men)

Commander:
Général de division
Roguet & staff

2nd Division of the Guard

2nd Brigade

3rd Brigade

Medical Service

Général de brigade
Lanabere & Colonel
Darriule & staff

1st Regiment de Tirailleurs
(320 officers & men)

Général de brigade
Boyledieu & Colonel
Vrigny

Regiment de Fusilier-Chasseurs
(320 officers & men)

Ambulance Company of the Guard

Colonel
Mallet & staff

1st Regiment de Voltigeurs
(300 officers & men)

Colonel
Bodelin
& staff

Regiment de Fusilier-Grenadiers
(320 officers & men)

Artillery

Colonel
Villeneuve
& staff

3rd Coy. (Young) Guard Artillerie à Pied (6 x
6 pdrs, 2 x 5-7" howitzers, 81 officers & men)

2nd Coy. Guard Train Regiment (65 officers & men)

Imperial Guard

Commander:
Général de division
Sorbier & staff

Guard Reserve Artillery

4th Coy. (Old) Guard Artillerie à Pied (6 x 6 pdrs, 2 x 5-7" howitzers, 95 officers & men)

Det. Coy. 1st Guard Train Regiment (85 officers & men)

5th Coy. (Old) Guard Artillerie à Pied (6 x 6 pdrs, 2 x 5-7" howitzers, 95 officers & men)

Det. Coy. 1st Guard Train Regiment (85 officers & men)

6th Coy. (Old) Guard Artillerie à Pied (6 x 6 pdrs, 2 x 5-7" howitzers, 95 officers & men)

Det. Coy. 2nd Guard Train Regiment (85 officers & men)

3rd Coy. (Old) Guard Artillerie à Cheval (4 x 6 pdrs, 2 x 5.7" howitzers, 65 officers & men)

Det. Coy. 2nd Guard Train Regiment (85 officers & men)

4th Coy. (Old) Guard Artillerie à Cheval (4 x 6 pdrs, 2 x 5.7" howitzers, 65 officers & men)

Det. Coy. 2nd Guard Train Regiment (85 officers & men)

Transport & Supply

Coy. Guard Equipage Train Battalion

Guard Dismounted Cavalry

Colonel Daulancourt & Chef d'escadron

Empress Dragoon Regiment (Old Guard) (380 officers & men)

Grenadiers à Cheval de la Garde (Old Guard) (400 officers & men)

Chef d'escadron

Chef d'escadron

Chasseurs à Cheval de la Garde (Old Guard) (400 officers & men)

2nd Chevauléger-lancier Regiment (340 officers & men)

Chef d'escadron

Chef d'escadron

1st Chevauléger-lancier Regiment (360 officers & men)

Chef d'escadron

Gendarmerie d'Elite (120 officers & men)

Imperial Guard Cavalry

 Commander: Maréchal Bessieres

 ADCs to Maréchal Bessieres

 Chief of staff: Général de brigade & staff

 Commander: Général de division Walther & staff

1st Division

1st Brigade

 Commander: Général de brigade St. Sulpice & staff

 Colonel Letort & staff

Empress Dragoon Regiment (Old Guard) (2 sqns. 420 officers & men)

 Général de brigade Lepic

Grenadiers à Cheval de la Garde (Old Guard) (2 sqns. 450 officers & men)

 Commander: Général de division Lefevbre-Desnouettes & staff

2nd Brigade

 Général de brigade Guyot

Chasseurs à Cheval de la Garde (Old Guard) (2 sqns. 450 officers & men)

 Chef de Escadron Karmann & Squadron de Mamelukes (Old Guard) (1 coy. 40 officers & men)

Imperial Guard Cavalry

1st Division

Commander:
Général de brigade
Colbert & staff

3rd Brigade

Colonel
Dotancourt

1st Chevauléger-lancier Regiment (2 sqns. 305 officers & men)

Colonel Dubya
de Ferrier

2nd Chevauléger-lancier Regiment (2 sqns. 275 officers & men)

Colonel Henri
& staff

Gendarmerie
d'Elite (1 sqn. 60
officers & men)

Artillery

Commander:
General de
brigade Desvaux
de St. Maurice
& staff

1st Coy. (Old) Guard Artillerie à Cheval (4 x 6
pdrs, 2 x 5.7" howitzers, 65 officers & men)

2nd Coy. (Old) Guard Artillerie à Cheval (4 x 6
pdrs, 2 x 5.7" howitzers, 62 officers & men)

2nd Coy. 7th Principal Train Battalion (50 officers & men)

3rd Coy. 7th Principal Train Battalion (50 officers & men)

I Army Corps

Commander:
Maréchal Davout

ADCs to
Maréchal Davout

Chief of staff: Général
de brigade Romeuf
& staff

1st to 4th Divisions

Général de division Morand & the Combined
13th Regt. de Légère, 17th & 30th de Ligne
(300 officers & men)

Général de brigade van Dedem de
Gelder & the Combined 15th Regt.
de Légère, 33rd & 48th de Ligne and
Joseph Napoleon Regt.
(250 officers & men)

Général de division Gérard & the
Combined 7th Regiment de Légère,
12th, 21st & 127th de Ligne
(200 officers & men)

Général de division Friederichs &
the Combined 35th Regiment de
Légère, 85th & 108th de Ligne
(150 officers & men)

5th Division

    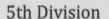

Général de
division
Compans &
staff

Combined battalions, 25th Regiment
de Ligne (300 officers & men)

Combined battalions, 57th Regiment
de Ligne (300 officers & men)

Combined battalions, 61st Regiment
de Ligne (300 officers & men)

Artillery

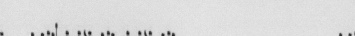

Chef de btn.
& staff

Combined coys. 7th Artillerie à
Pied (6 x 6 pdrs, 2 x 24 pdr
howitzers, 92 officers & men)

Combined coys. 7th Artillerie à
Pied (6 x 6 pdrs, 2 x 24 pdr
howitzers, 92 officers & men)

Combined coys. 1st, 3rd & 6th
Artillerie à Cheval (4 x 6 pdrs, 2 x 24
pdr howitzers, 91 officers & men)

Combined coys. 1st Principal Train Battalion
(75 officers & men)

Combined coys. 1st Principal Train Battalion
(75 officers & men)

Combined coys. 1st & 9th Principal Train Battalions
(75 officers & men)

Transport & Supply

Combined coys. Military Equipage Battalion

Medical Service

Ambulance Company

II Army Corps

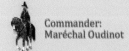 Commander: Maréchal Oudinot

 ADCs to Maréchal Oudinot

 Chief of staff: Général de brigade Latrille de Lorencez & staff

 Commander: Général de division Legrand & staff

6th Division

 Commander: Général de brigade Albert & staff

1st Brigade

 Commander: Général de brigade Moreau & staff

2nd Brigade

Artillery

 Colonel Gucheneuc & staff

 1st Battalion 26th Regiment de Légère (188 officers & men)

 2nd Battalion 26th Regiment de Légère (188 officers & men)

 3rd Battalion 26th Regiment de Légère (188 officers & men)

 4th Battalion 26th Regiment de Légère (188 officers & men)

 Colonel Lejeune & staff

 1st Battalion 56th Regiment de Ligne (188 officers & men)

 2nd Battalion 56th Regiment de Ligne (188 officers & men)

 3rd Battalion 56th Regiment de Ligne (188 officers & men)

 4th Battalion 56th Regiment de Ligne (188 officers & men)

 Chef de bataillon & staff — 11th Coy. 5th Artillerie à Pied (6 x 6 pdrs, 2 x 24 pdr howitzers, 98 officers & men)

 3rd Coy. 3rd Principal Train Battalion (75 officers & men)

Transport & Supply

Medical Service

Company, Military Equipage Battalion

Company, Military Equipage Battalion

Ambulance Company

II Army Corps

Commander: Général de brigade Maison & staff

3rd Brigade

Colonel Aubry & staff

1st Battalion 19th Regiment de Ligne (188 officers & men)

2nd Battalion 19th Regiment de Ligne (188 officers & men)

3rd Battalion 19th Regiment de Ligne (188 officers & men)

4th Battalion 19th Regiment de Ligne (188 officers & men)

6th Division

Commander: Général de brigade Pamplona & staff

4th Brigade

Colonel Melzinger & staff

1st Battalion 128th (Bremen) Regiment de Ligne (188 officers & men)

2nd Battalion 128th (Bremen) Regiment de Ligne (188 officers & men)

Colonel Montigny & staff

1st Battalion, 3rd Regiment, Portuguese Legion (188 officers & men)

2nd Battalion, 3rd Regiment, Portuguese Legion (188 officers & men)

Artillery

6th Coy. 3rd Artillerie à Cheval (4 x 6 pdrs, 2 x 24 pdr howitzers, 72 officers & men)

1st & 3rd Coys. 3rd Principal Train Battalion (65 officers & men)

Transport & Supply

Company, Military Equipage Battalion

Company, Military Equipage Battalion

Medical Service

Ambulance Company

II Army Corps

8th Division

Commander:
Général de division
Verdier & staff

Commander: Général
de brigade Raymond-
Vivies & staff

1st Brigade

Colonel
Casabianca
& staff

1st Battalion 11th
Regiment de Légère
(188 officers & men)

2nd Battalion 11th
Regiment de Légère
(188 officers & men)

3rd Battalion 11th
Regiment de Légère
(188 officers & men)

4th Battalion 11th
Regiment de Légère
(188 officers & men)

Colonel De
Wimpfen
& staff

1st Battalion 2nd
Regiment de Ligne
(188 officers & men)

2nd Battalion 2nd
Regiment de Ligne
(188 officers & men)

3rd Battalion 2nd
Regiment de Ligne
(188 officers & men)

4th Battalion 2nd
Regiment de Ligne
(188 officers & men)

6th Battalion 2nd
Regiment de Ligne
(188 officers & men)

Artillery

15th Coy. 5th Artillerie à Pied (6
x 6 pdrs, 2 x 24 pdr howitzers,
98 officers & men)

1st Coy. 3rd Principal Train Battalion
(75 officers & men)

Transport & Supply

Company, Military Equipage Battalion

Company, Military Equipage
Battalion

Medical Service

Ambulance Company

II Army Corps

8th Division

Commander:
Général de
brigade Pouget
& staff

2nd Brigade

Colonel Mayot
& staff

1st Battalion 37th
Regiment de Ligne
(188 officers & men)

2nd Battalion 37th
Regiment de Ligne
(188 officers & men)

Colonel Hardyau
& staff

1st Battalion 124th
(Dutch) Regt. de Ligne
(188 officers & men)

2nd Battalion 124th
(Dutch) Regt. de Ligne
(188 officers & men)

Artillery

1st Coy. 3rd Artillerie à Cheval (4 x 6 pdrs,
2 x 24 pdr howitzers, 72 officers & men)

3rd Battalion 37th
Regiment de Ligne
(188 officers & men)

4th Battalion 37th
Regiment de Ligne
(188 officers & men)

3rd Battalion 124th
(Dutch) Regt. de Ligne
(188 officers & men)

5th Coy. 3rd Principal Train Battalion (65 officers & men)

Transport & Supply

Company, Military Equipage Battalion

Medical Service

Ambulance Company

II Army Corps

9th Division

Commander:
Général de
division Merle
& staff

Commander:
Général de
brigade Amey
& staff

1st Brigade

Commander:
Général de
brigade Condras
& staff

2nd Brigade

Colonel D'Affry
& staff

1st Battalion, 4th Swiss
Infantry Regiment
(188 officers & men)

2nd Battalion, 4th Swiss
Infantry Regiment
(188 officers & men)

3rd Battalion, 4th Swiss
Infantry Regiment
(188 officers & men)

Colonel Raquetly
& staff

1st Battalion, 1st Swiss
Infantry Regiment
(188 officers & men)

2nd Battalion, 1st Swiss
Infantry Regiment
(188 officers & men)

Colonel Joly
& staff

1st Battalion, 3rd
Provisional Croatian
Infantry Regiment
(188 officers & men)

2nd Battalion, 3rd
Provisional Croatian
Infantry Regiment
(188 officers & men)

Colonel Castella
de Berlens & staff

1st Battalion, 2nd Swiss
Infantry Regiment
(188 officers & men)

2nd Battalion, 2nd Swiss
Infantry Regiment
(188 officers & men)

3rd Battalion, 2nd Swiss
Infantry Regiment
(188 officers & men)

Transport & Supply

Company, Military Equipage Battalion

Medical Service

Ambulance Company

II Army Corps

9th Division

Commander: Général de brigade Coustard & staff

3rd Brigade

Colonel Thomasset & staff

1st Battalion, 3rd Swiss Infantry Regiment (188 officers & men)

2nd Battalion, 3rd Swiss Infantry Regiment (188 officers & men)

3rd Battalion, 3rd Swiss Infantry Regiment (188 officers & men)

Colonel Avizard & staff

1st Battalion 123rd (Dutch) Regt. de Ligne (200 officers & men)

2nd Battalion 123rd (Dutch) Regt. de Ligne (200 officers & men)

3rd Battalion 123rd (Dutch) Regt. de Ligne (200 officers & men)

4th Battalion 123rd (Dutch) Regt. de Ligne (200 officers & men)

Artillery

4th Coy.7th Artillerie à Pied (6 x 6 pdrs, 2 x 24 pdr howitzers, 98 officers & men)

3rd Coy. 8th Principal Train Battalion (75 officers & men)

5th Coy. 2nd Artillerie à Cheval (4 x 6 pdrs, 2 x 24 pdr howitzers, 72 officers & men)

5th Coy. 8th Principal Train Battalion (65 officers & men)

Transport, Supply & Medical Service

Company, Military Equipage Battalion

Ambulance Company

II Army Corps

Commander:
Général de
brigade Castex
& staff

5th Light Cavalry Brigade

Colonel Marbot
& staff

23rd Regiment de Chasseurs à Cheval (4 sqns. 500 officers & men)

Colonel Amiel
& staff

24th Regiment de Chasseurs à Cheval (4 sqns. 360 officers & men)

Général de brigade
Corbineau & staff

6th Light Cavalry Brigade

Attached Cavalry

Colonel De Saint-
Chamans & staff

7th Regiment de Chasseurs à Cheval
(2 sqns. 140 officers & men)

Colonel Piasecki
& staff

2nd Polish Uhlan Regiment
(1 sqn.125 officers & men)

Colonel Zawadzki
& staff

7th Polish Uhlan Regiment
(1 sqn.125 officers & men)

Chef d'escadron
Sourd & staff

20th Regiment de Chasseurs à Cheval
(2 sqns. 140 officers & men)

Colonel Lagouski
& staff

8th Polish Uhlan Regiment
(1 sqn.120 officers & men)

Colonel
Przezdziecki
& staff

18th Lithuanian Uhlans
(1 sqn. 85 officers & men)

Colonel Lubienski
& staff

8th (Vistula) Regiment de Chevau-Léger
Lanciers (2 sqns. 120 officers & men)

Colonel Rajecki
& staff

19th Lithuanian Uhlans
(1 sqn. 110 officers & men)

II Army Corps

Commander:
Général de division
Chasseloup-Laubat
& staff

Sappers

Sapper's Train

Chef de btn.
& staff

5th Coy. 1st Sapper Btn. (95 officers & men)
3rd Coy. 3rd Sapper Btn. (95 officers & men)
4th Coy. 3rd Sapper Btn. (95 officers & men)

Général de
division
Kirgener

Sapper Coy (80 officers &
men) & Ouvriers Coy of the
Guard (64 officers & men)

5th Coy. Polish Sapper Btn. (80 officers & men)
Coy. Spanish Sappers (80 officers & men)
l'ile d'Elbe Sappers (2 coys, 95 officers & men)

Capitaine de
Vaisseau
Ganteaume
& staff

6th & 7th Coys. Guard
Marine Btn.
(160 officers & men)

Chef de btn.
Blaux & staff

Coy. Berg Sappers
(190 officers & men)

Coy. Sappers Equipment Train (95 officers & men)

Equipage Coy. Old Guard Sappers (60 officers & men)
Equipage Coy. Berg Sappers (40 officers & men)

Commander:
Général de
division Eblé
& staff

Pontoniers

Chef de btn.
Gauthier & staff

1st Pononier Btn.
(2nd, 7th and 9th
coys, 175 officers
& men)

Chef de btn.
Chapelle & staff

2nd Pononier Btn. (2nd,
3rd, 4th & 5th coys, 225
officers & men)

Pontonier's
Train

Coy. Pontoniers Equipment Train (85 officers & men)

IV Army Corps

 Commander:
Prince Eugene de
Beauharnais, Viceroy
of Italy

 ADCs to
Prince Eugene
de Beauharnais

 Chief of Staff:
Général de brigade
Guilleminot & staff

 Colonel Pégot
& staff, 84th
de Ligne

 Colonel Ricard & the
8th Regiment de Légère
(125 officers & men)

Chef de btn. & the
84th Regiment de Ligne
(140 officers & men)

Major Tissot & the 92nd
Regiment de Ligne (100
officers & men)

13th Division

 Général de
division
Broussier & staff

 Colonel Gaussart & the
18th Regiment de Légère
(165 officers & men)

Colonel Vautré & the 9th
Regiment de Ligne
(125 officers & men)

 Colonel Figie & the 35th
Regiment de Ligne
(150 officers & men)

14th Division

 Colonel Bertrand & the
106th Regiemnt de Ligne
(95 officers & men)

 Colonel Marko Šljivaric
& the 1st Croatian
Infantry Regiment
(110 officers & men)

 Colonel Grobon & the 53rd
Regiment de Ligne
(135 officers & men)

 Major Dorey & the Joseph
Napoleon Regiment
(130 officers & men)

 Général de
brigade Lechi
& staff

 Combined Royal Velites, Guard
Infantry and Conscript Guards
(300 officers & men)

Italian Royal Guard & Dismounted Cavalry

 Chef de btn.
& staff

 Combined Artillery Companies (10 guns of
mixed calibre, 150 officers & men)

Artillery

 Chef d'escadron
& staff

Combined French Chasseurs
& Bavarian Chevau-Légers
(300 officers & men)

 Combined Artillery Train Companies (110 officers & men)

Transport & Supply

Medical Service

 Company, Military Equipage Battalion

 Ambulance Company

III Army Corps

 Commander: Maréchal Ney

 ADCs to Maréchal Ney

 Chief of staff: Général de brigade Gouré & staff

 Commander: Général de division Ledru & staff

10th Division

1st Brigade

2nd Brigade

Général de brigade Gengoult

Colonel de Julienne de Bellair & 1st Combined Battalion, 24th Regiment de Légère

2nd Combined Battalion, 24th Regiment de Légère (160 officers & men)

Colonel Freire-Pégo & the 1st Regt, Portuguse Legion (120 officers & men)

Commander: Colonel Brue, 46th de Ligne

Chef de btn. & 1st Combined Btn, 46th Regt. de Ligne (150 officers & men)

2nd Combined Btn, 46th Regt. de Ligne (150 officers & men)

3rd Brigade

Général de brigade Bruny

Colonel Lafitte & 1st Combined Battalion, 72nd Regiment de Ligne (200 officers & men)

2nd Combined Battalion, 72nd Regiment de Ligne (175 officers & men)

Colonel Freytag & the 129th (Oldenburg) Regiment de Ligne (125 officers & men)

Artillery

Medical Service

Ambulance Company

Chef de btn. Ragmey & staff

12th Coy. 5th Artillerie à Pied (6 x 6 pdrs, 2 x 24 pdr howitzers, 85 officers & men)

5th Coy. 6th Artillerie à Cheval (4 x 6 pdrs, 2 x 24 pdr howitzers, 34 officers & men)

1st Coy. 6th Principal Train Battalion (85 officers & men)

2nd Coy. 6th Principal Train Battalion (45 officers & men)

III Army Corps

11th Division

Général de brigade d'Henin & staff

4th (80 men) 18th (100 men) 93rd (100 men) de Ligne & 2nd Portuguese (30 men)

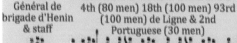

Chef de btn. Bernard & staff

Combined 18th Coy. 5th Artillerie à Pied & 6th Coy. 6th Art. à Cheval (10 gun. 130 officers & men)

Artillery

Combined 3rd & 4th Coya. 6th Principal Train Battalion (65 officers & men)

25th (Württemberg) Division

Général de division Marchand & staff

Combined Württemberg Regiments (2 battalions 300 officers & men)

Oberstleutnant von Brandt

Combined 1st Coy. Württemberg Foot & 1st Coy, Horse Art. (9 guns, 98 officers & men)

Artillery

Coy, Württemberg Artillery Train (60 officers & men)

3rd Cuirassier Division

Commander: Général de division Doumerc & staff

Colonel Dujon & staff

4th Regiment de Cuirassiers (165 officers & men)

Colonel Dubois & staff

7th Regiment de Cuirassiers (165 officers & men)

Colonel Trip & staff

14th Regiment de Cuirassiers (162 officers & men)

Artillery

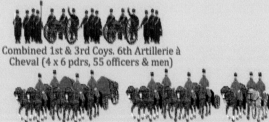

Combined 1st & 3rd Coys. 6th Artillerie à Cheval (4 x 6 pdrs, 55 officers & men)

Combined 2nd & 6th Coya. 11th Principal Train Battalion (36 officers & men)

Transport, Supply & Medical Service

Company, Military Equipage Battalion

Ambulance Company

V Army Corps

Commander: Général de division Zajaczek & staff

16th Division

Commander: Général de brigade Paszkowski & staff

1st Brigade

Général de brigade Mielzynski & staff

Colonel Blumer

1st Btn, 3rd Polish Infantry Regt. (180 officers & men)

2nd Btn, 3rd Polish Infantry Regt. (180 officers & men)

Major Rybinski

1st Btn, 15th Polish Infantry Regt. (140 officers & men)

2nd Btn, 15th Polish Infantry Regt. (140 officers & men)

2nd Brigade

Général de brigade Paszkowski & staff

Colonel Prince Czartorisky

1st Btn, 16th Polish Infantry Regt. (160 officers & men)

2nd Btn, 16th Polish Infantry Regt. (160 officers & men)

Chef de bataillon Sowinski

Combined 3rd & 12th Coys. Polish Foot Artillery Regiment (4 x 6 pdrs, 2 x 24 pdr howitzers, 86 officers & men)

Transport & Supply

Company, Polish Equipment Train

Artillery

Combined coys. Polish Artillery Train Battalion (65 officers & men)

17th Division

Commander: Général de brigade Kniaziewicz & staff

1st Brigade

Général de brigade Zoltowski

Colonel Małachowski & the 1st Polish Infantry Regiment (240 officers & men)

Colonel Sierawski & the 6th Polish Infantry Regiment (240 officers & men)

2nd Brigade

Général de brigade Pakosz

Colonel Siemianowski & the 14th Polish Infantry Regiment (200 officers & men)

Colonel Hornowski & the 17th Polish Infantry Regiment (200 officers & men)

Artillery

Major Gugenmus

11th Coy. Polish Foot Artillery Regiment (4 x 6 pdrs, 2 x 24 pdr howitzers, 86 officers & men)

Combined coys. Polish Artillery Train Battalion (65 officers & men)

Transport & Supply

Company, Polish Equipment Train

V Army Corps

Commander:
Général de division
Krasinski & staff

18th Division

1st Brigade

Général de brigade Pototzki

Colonel Krukowiecki & 1st Btn, 2nd Polish Infantry Regt. (160 officers & men)

2nd Btn, 2nd Polish Infantry Regt. (160 officers & men)

Colonel Stuart & 1st Btn, 8th Polish Infantry Regt. (160 officers & men)

2nd Btn, 8th Polish Infantry Regt. (160 officers & men)

Colonel Wiezbinski & 1st Btn, 12th Polish Infantry Regt. (180 officers & men)

2nd Btn, 12th Polish Infantry Regt. (180 officers & men)

Chef de btn Ushinski

Combined 4th & 5th Coys. Polish Foot Artillery Regiment (4 x 6 pdrs, 2 x 24 pdr howitzers, 90 officers & men)

Transport & Supply

Company, Polish Equipment Train

Artillery

Combined coys. Polish Artillery Train Battalion (65 officers & men)

Commander:
Général de division
Claparede & staff

The Vistula Legion (attached)

1st Brigade

Général de brigade Cholpicki

Colonel Konsinovski

1st Btn, 1st Infantry Regt., Vistula Legion (300 officers & men)

2nd Btn, 1st Infantry Regt., Vistula Legion (300 officers & men)

Colonel Malchevski

1st Btn, 2nd Infantry Regt., Vistula Legion (300 officers & men)

2nd Btn, 2nd Infantry Regt., Vistula Legion (300 officers & men)

2nd Brigade

Général de brigade Bronikowski

Colonel Fondzelski

1st Btn, 3rd Infantry Regt., Vistula Legion (300 officers & men)

2nd Btn, 3rd Infantry Regt., Vistula Legion (300 officers & men)

Artillery

Captain Fradiel

13th Coy. 8th Artillerie à Pied (6 x 6 pdrs, 2 x 24 pdr howitzers, 93 officers & men)

6th Coy. 4th Principal Train Battalion (98 officers & men)

VIII Army Corps

Commander:
Général de
division Junot

ADCs to
Général de
division Junot

Chief of Staff:
Colonel Revest
& staff

Artillery: Général
de division Allix
de Vaux & staff

23rd Division

Commander:
Oberst von
Fullgraf & staff

Oberstleutnant von
Hessberg & 3rd Westphalian
Light Infantry Battalion
(120 officers & men)

Oberstlieutnant Wetzel & the 2nd & 6th
Westphalian Line Infantry Regiments
(220 officers & men)

Oberst Bernard & the 3rd & 7th
Westphalian Line Infantry
Regiments (180 officers & men)

24th Division

Commander:
Generalleutnant
von Ochs & staff

Major Muldner & the Westphalian
Grenadier-Garde Battalion
(200 officers & men)

Major von Raushenplatt & the 1st
Westphalian Light Infantry Battalion
(150 officers & men)

Chef de bataillon von Stein & the
Westphalian Garde Chasseur-Carabiniers
Battalion (200 officers & men)

Major Picot & the Westphalian
Garde Chasseur Battalion
(200 officers & men)

Oberst Gissot & the 5th Westphalian
Line Infantry Regiment
(200 officers & men)

24th Light Cavalry Brigade

Generalmajor von
Hammerstein
& staff

Combined Westphalian Husaren
Regiments (120 officers & men)

Transport & Supply

Westphalian Military Equipage Company

IX Army Corps

 Commander: Maréchal Victor

 ADCs to Maréchal Victor

 Chief of Staff: Commandant D'Arcy & staff

 Artillery: Colonel Caron & staff

 Engineers: Colonel Bigot-Charmoy & staff

 Commander: Général de division Daendels & staff

26th Division

 Commander: Général de brigade Damas & staff

1st (Berg) Brigade

 Commander: Général de brigade Lingg & staff

2nd (Berg) Brigade

 Oberst Genty & staff

1st Battalion, 1st Berg Infantry Regiment
(480 officers & men)

2nd Battalion, 1st Berg Infantry Regiment
(480 officers & men)

 Oberst Forch & staff

1st Battalion, 4th Berg Infantry Regiment
(480 officers & men)

2nd Battalion, 4th Berg Infantry Regiment
(480 officers & men)

 Oberst Hoffmeyer & staff

1st Battalion, 2nd Berg Infantry Regiment
(480 officers & men)

2nd Battalion, 2nd Berg Infantry Regiment
(480 officers & men)

 Oberst Boisdavid & staff

1st Battalion, 3rd Berg Infantry Regiment
(480 officers & men)

2nd Battalion, 3rd Berg Infantry Regiment
(480 officers & men)

IX Army Corps

26th Division

3rd (Baden) Brigade

Commander:
Generalmajor
Hochberg & staff

Oberst Van
Francken & staff

1st Battalion, 1st (Leib) Infantry Regiment
(480 officers & men)

Oberst Bruckner
& staff

1st Battalion, 3rd (Hochberg) Infantry Regiment
(480 officers & men)

Major & staff

1st (Lingg) Baden Jäger Battalion
(480 officers & men)

2nd Battalion, 1st (Leib) Infantry Regiment
(480 officers & men)

2nd Battalion, 3rd (Hochberg) Infantry Regiment
(480 officers & men)

Transport & Supply

Artillery

Oberstleutnant
Bogaert & staff

Berg Foot Artillery Battery (6 x 6 pdr cannons,
2 x 24 pdr howitzers, 100 officers & men)

Berg Horse Artillery Battery (4 x 6 pdr cannons,
2 x 24 pdr howitzers, 80 officers & men)

Berg Military Equipage Company

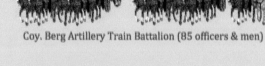

Coy. Berg Artillery Train Battalion (85 officers & men)

Coy. Berg Artillery Train Battalion (65 officers & men)

Baden Foot Artillery Battery (4 x 6 pdr
cannons, 65 officers & men)

Baden Horse Artillery Battery (4 x 6 pdr
cannons, 50 officers & men)

Baden Military Equipage Company

Coy. Baden Artillery Train Battalion (55 officers & men)

Coy. Baden Artillery Train Battalion (45 officers & men)

IX Army Corps

28th Division

1st (Polish) Brigade

Commander: Général de division Girard & staff

Commander: General de brigade Ouviller & staff

Colonel Żdzitowiecki & staff

1st Battalion, 4th Polish Iinfantry Regiment (480 officers & men)

Colonel Oranowski & staff

1st Battalion, 7th Polish Iinfantry Regiment (480 officers & men)

Colonel Cicoski & staff

1st Battalion, 9th Polish Iinfantry Regiment (480 officers & men)

2nd Battalion, 4th Polish Iinfantry Regiment (480 officers & men)

2nd Battalion, 7th Polish Iinfantry Regiment (480 officers & men)

2nd Battalion, 9th Polish Iinfantry Regiment (480 officers & men)

Artillery

1st Coy. Polish Foot Artillery Regiment (4 x 6 pdrs, 2 x 24 pdr howitzers, 80 officers & men)

2nd Coy. Polish Foot Artillery Regiment (4 x 6 pdrs, 2 x 24 pdr howitzers, 80 officers & men)

Coy. Polish Artillery Train Battalion (65 officers & men)

Coy. Polish Artillery Train Battalion (65 officers & men)

IX Army Corps

28th Division

Commamder: Generalmajor Klengel & staff

2nd (Saxon) Brigade

Transport & Supply

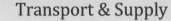

Oberst & staff

1st Battalion, von Low Infantry Regiment
(480 officers & men)

Oberst & staff

1st Battalion, von Rechten Infantry Regiment
(480 officers & men)

Coy. Polish Equipment Train

2nd Battalion, von Low Infantry Regiment
(480 officers & men)

2nd Battalion, von Rechten Infantry Regiment
(480 officers & men)

Coy. Polish Equipment Train

Commander: General de brigade Fournier-Sarlovèze & staff

Cavalry (from 30th & 31st Brigades)

Général de division Lorge & staff

7th Cuirassier Division (attached)

Oberst Laroche-Starkenfels & staff

Baden Hussar Regiment (2 sqns. 180 officers & men)

Combined Saxon and Westhalian Cuirassiers
(150 officers & men)

Oberst Dalwigk & staff

Hessian Garde Chevauleger Regiment (2 sqns. 170 officers & men)

Russian Armies - Right Wing

Commander:
General of Cavalry
Wittgenstein

ADCs to
General of Cavalry
Wittgenstein

Chief of Staff:
Generalmajor
D'Auvray & staff

Quartermaster-
General: Colonel
Diebitsch & staff

Vanguard

Colonel & staff

1st Platov Don Cossack Regiment (4 sotns. 336 officers & men)

Colonel & staff

Grodno Hussar Regiment (8 sqns. 1,044 officers & men)

Artillery

23rd Horse Battery (8 x 6 pdrs, 102 officers & men)

Right Wing

Vanguard

Colonel & staff

1st Battalion, 24th Jäger Regiment (669 officers & men)

3rd Battalion, 24th Jäger Regiment (669 officers & men)

Colonel & staff

1st Battalion, 25th Jäger Regiment (669 officers & men)

3rd Battalion, 25th Jäger Regiment (669 officers & men)

Artillery

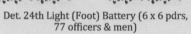

Det. 24th Light (Foot) Battery (6 x 6 pdrs, 77 officers & men)

Transport & Supply

Company, Equipment Train

Medical Service

Ambulance Company

Right Wing

5th Infantry Division

Commander:
Generalmajor
Berg & staff

Colonel & staff

1st Battalion, Perm Infantry Regiment (608 officers & men)

Colonel & staff

1st Battalion, Mohilev Infantry Regiment (618 officers & men)

3rd Battalion, Perm Infantry Regiment (607 officers & men)

3rd Battalion, Mohilev Infantry Regiment (617 officers & men)

Colonel & staff

1st Battalion, 23rd Jäger Regiment (643 officers & men)

3rd Battalion, 23rd Jäger Regiment (642 officers & men)

Artillery

Transport & Supply

Colonel & staff

Company, Equipment Train

3rd Position (Foot) Battery (8 x 12 pdrs, 4 x 20 pdr unicorns, 213 officers & men)

6th Light (Foot) Battery (6 x 6 pdrs, 6 x 10 pdr unicorns, 141 officers & men)

Medical Service

Ambulance Company

11th Reserve (Foot) Battery (8 x 12 pdrs, 4 x 20 pdr unicorns, 240 officers & men)

36th Reserve (Foot) Battery (8 x 12 pdrs, 4 x 20 pdr unicorns, 234 officers & men)

Right Wing

Grenadier Division

Commander:
Generalmajor
Hamen & staff

Colonel & staff

1st Battalion, Tauride Grenadier Regiment
(302 officers & men)

Colonel & staff

1st Battalion, Pavlovski Grenadier Regiment
(363 officers & men)

Colonel & staff

1st Battalion, Saint-Petersburg Grenadier
Regiment (357 officers & men)

Colonel & staff

1st Battalion, Ekaterinoslav Grenadier
Regiment (363 officers & men)

Colonel & staff

1st Battalion, Araktscheyev Grenadier
Regiment (267 officers & men)

Lt. Colonel & staff

1st Battalion, Combined Grenadiers of 5th Division
(508 officers & men)

Lt. Colonel & staff

1st Battalion, Combined Grenadiers of 14th Division
(486 officers & men)

2nd Battalion, Combined Grenadiers of 5th Division
(508 officers & men)

2nd Battalion, Combined Grenadiers of 14th Division
(486 officers & men)

Major & staff

Depot Battalion, Corps Grenadiers
(288 officers & men)

Transport
& Supply

Medical
Service

Company, Equipment Train

Ambulance Company

Right Wing

Cavalry (attached)

Colonel & staff

Iamberg Dragoon Regiment (4 sqns. 409 officers & men)

Artillery

3rd Horse Battery (8 x 6 pdrs, 4 x 10 pdr Licornes, 213 officers & men)

Commander:
Generalmajor
Balk & staff

Cavalry Division

Colonel & staff

Riga Dragoon Regiment (4 sqns. 500 officers & men)

Artillery

1st Horse Battery (8 x 6 pdrs, 4 x 10 pdr Licornes, 216 officers & men)

Right Wing

14th Division (Reserve)

Commander:
Generalleutnant
Sasonov & staff

1st Brigade

Commander:
Generalmajor
& staff

Colonel & staff

1st Battalion, Toula Infantry Regiment (578 officers & men)

Colonel & staff

1st Battalion, Navaginsk Infantry Regiment (563 officers & men)

3rd Battalion, Toula Infantry Regiment (578 officers & men)

3rd Battalion, Navaginsk Infantry Regiment (563 officers & men)

Colonel & staff

1st Battalion, 26th Jäger Regiment (622 officers & men)

3rd Battalion, 26th Jäger Regiment (621 officers & men)

Major & staff

Det. 3rd Position (Foot) Battery (6 x 12 pdrs, 4 x
20 pdr unicorns, 156 officers & men)

Coy. Pioneers
(93 officers & men)

Artillery
& Pioneers

6th Light (Foot) Battery (6 x 6 pdrs, 6 x 10 pdr
unicorns, 160 officers & men)

Right Wing

Commander:
Generalmajor
& staff

14th Division (Reserve)

2nd Brigade

Colonel & staff

1st Battalion, Tenguinsk Infantry Regiment (602 officers & men)

Colonel & staff

1st Battalion, Estonia Infantry Regiment (616 officers & men)

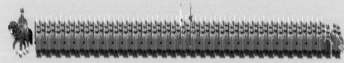

3rd Battalion, Tenguinsk Infantry Regiment (602 officers & men)

3rd Battalion, Estonia Infantry Regiment (615 officers & men)

Commander:
Generalmajor
Repnin & staff

Cavalry Brigade

Major & staff

Depot Sqn. Chevalier-Garde Regiment (1 sqn. 200 officers & men)

Major & staff

Reserve Sqn. Garde Hussar Regiment
(1 sqn. 144 officers & men)

Depot Sqn. Emperor's Cuirassier Regiment (1 sqn. 200 officers & men)

Reserve Sqn. Garde Uhlan Regiment
(1 sqn. 130 officers & men)

Depot Sqn. Empress's Cuirassier Regiment
(1 sqn. 133 officers & men)

Reserve Sqn. Garde Dragoon Regiment
(1 sqn. 130 officers & men)

Artillery

14th Position (Foot) Battery (8 x 12 pdrs, 4 x 20 pdr unicorns, 233 officers & men)

Army of Finland

 Commander:
Generalleutnant
Steinheil

 ADCs to
Generalleutnant
Steinheil

 Chief of Staff:
Generalmajor
& staff

6th Infantry Division

  Commander:
Generalmajor
Rachmanov
& staff

 Commander:
Generalmajor
Gorbuntsov
& staff

1st Brigade

 Commander:
Generalmajor
Nilus & staff

2nd Brigade

 Major
Bogdanovich
& staff

 1st Battalion, Briansk Infantry
Regiment (264 officers & men)

 3rd Battalion, Briansk Infantry
Regiment (264 officers & men)

 Major Andreev
& staff

 1st Battalion, Uglich Infantry
Regiment (264 officers & men)

 3rd Battalion, Uglich Infantry
Regiment (264 officers & men)

 Lt. Colonel
Bazin & staff

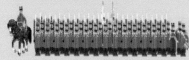 1st Battalion, Nizov Infantry Regiment
(264 officers & men)

 3rd Battalion, Nizov Infantry
Regiment (264 officers & men)

 Major Melgunov
& staff

 1st Battalion, 35th Jäger Regiment
(264 officers & men)

 3rd Battalion, 35th Jäger Regiment
(264 officers & men)

Transport & Supply

Company, Equipment Train

Medical Service

Ambulance Company

Army of Finland

6th Infantry Division

3rd Brigade

Commander:
Colonel Treskin
& staff

Major Karm
& staff

1st Battalion, Azov Infantry
Regiment (264 officers & men)

3rd Battalion, Azov Infantry
Regiment (264 officers & men)

Colonel
Turchaninov
& staff

1st Battalion, 3rd Jäger Regiment
(264 officers & men)

3rd Battalion, 3rd Jäger Regiment
(264 officers & men)

Artillery

Colonel Shulman
& staff

6th Position (Foot) Battery (8 x 12 pdrs, 4 x 20 pdr
unicorns, 233 officers & men)

11th Light (Foot) Battery (6 x 6 pdrs, 6 x 10 pdr
unicorns, 160 officers & men)

Transport & Supply

Company, Equipment Train

Medical Service

Ambulance Company

Army of Finland

21st Infantry Division

Commander:
Generalmajor
Rosen & staff

Commander:
Colonel Maslov
& staff

1st Brigade

Commander:
Colonel Rosen
& staff

2nd Brigade

Lt. Colonel
Mendeleev & staff

1st Battalion, Podolsk Infantry
Regiment (264 officers & men)

3rd Battalion, Podolsk Infantry
Regiment (264 officers & men)

Colonel Sheele
& staff

1st Battalion, Nevaski Infantry
Regiment (264 officers & men)

3rd Battalion, Nevaski Infantry
Regiment (264 officers & men)

Major Sergeev
& staff

1st Battalion, Petrovski Infantry
Regiment (264 officers & men)

3rd Battalion, Petrovski Infantry
Regiment (264 officers & men)

Transport & Supply

Company, Equipment Train

Medical Service

Ambulance Company

Army of Finland

21st Infantry Division

Commander:
Colonel Kniper
& staff

3rd Brigade

Major Essen
& staff

1st Battalion, 2nd Jäger Regiment
(264 officers & men)

3rd Battalion, 2nd Jäger Regiment
(264 officers & men)

Colonel
Ridinger & staff

1st Battalion, 44th Jäger Regiment
(264 officers & men)

3rd Battalion, 44th Jäger Regiment
(264 officers & men)

Colonel Tretiakov
& staff

21st Position (Foot) Battery (8 x 12 pdrs, 4 x 20
pdr unicorns, 233 officers & men)

Artillery

40th Light (Foot) Battery (6 x 6 pdrs, 6 x 10 pdr
unicorns, 160 officers & men)

Transport & Supply

Company, Equipment Train

Medical Service

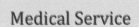

Ambulance Company

Army of Finland

25th Infantry Division

Commander:
Generalmajor
Gamen & staff

1st Brigade

Commander:
Colonel & staff

2nd Brigade

Commander:
Colonel & staff

Major & staff

1st Battalion, 1st Naval (Marine)
Infantry Regiment (264 officers & men)

3rd Battalion, 1st Naval (Marine)
Infantry Regiment (264 officers & men)

Major & staff

1st Battalion, 3rd Naval (Marine)
Infantry Regiment (264 officers & men)

3rd Battalion, 3rd Naval (Marine)
Infantry Regiment (264 officers & men)

Colonel & staff

1st Battalion, 2nd Naval (Marine)
Infantry Regiment (264 officers & men)

3rd Battalion, 2nd Naval (Marine)
Infantry Regiment (264 officers & men)

Colonel & staff

1st Battalion, Voronejki Infantry
Regiment (264 officers & men)

3rd Battalion, Voronejki Infantry
Regiment (264 officers & men)

Transport & Supply

Company, Equipment Train

Medical Service

Ambulance Company

Army of Finland

25th Infantry Division

Commander:
Colonel & staff

3rd Brigade

Major & staff

1st Battalion, 31st Jäger Regiment
(264 officers & men)

3rd Battalion, 31st Jäger Regiment
(264 officers & men)

Colonel & staff

1st Battalion, 47th Jäger Regiment
(264 officers & men)

3rd Battalion, 47th Jäger Regiment
(264 officers & men)

Artillery

Colonel & staff

25th Position (Foot) Battery (8 x 12 pdrs, 4 x 20
pdr unicorns, 233 officers & men)

49th Light (Foot) Battery (6 x 6 pdrs, 6 x 10 pdr
unicorns, 160 officers & men)

50th Horse Battery (8 x 6 pdrs, 4 x 10 pdr Licornes,
216 officers & men)

Transport & Supply

Company, Equipment Train

Medical Service

Ambulance Company

Army of Finland

Cavalry Brigade

Commander:
Generalmajor
& staff

Colonel & staff

Finland Dragoon Regiment (4 sqns. 300 officers & men)

Colonel & staff

Mitau Dragoon Regiment (4 sqns. 300 officers & men)

Colonel & staff

Poschilin Cossack Regiment (5 sotns. 300 officers & men)

Transport & Supply

Company, Equipment Train

Medical Service

Ambulance Company

Army of the Danube

Commander: Admiral Tchichagov

ADCs to Admiral Tchichagov

Chief of Staff: Generalleutnant Sabaneyev & staff

Duty General: Generalmajor Tuchkov & staff

Quartermaster-General: Generalmajor Berg & staff

Commander: Generalmajor Tchlapitz & staff

Vanguard (from 18th Division)

Artillery

Colonel & staff

1st Battalion, 28th Jäger Regiment (360 officers & men)

Colonel & staff

1st Battalion, 32nd Jäger Regiment (360 officers & men)

2nd Battalion, 28th Jäger Regiment (360 officers & men)

2nd Battalion, 32nd Jäger Regiment (360 officers & men)

13th Horse Battery (8 x 6 pdrs, 4 x 10 pdr Licornes, 216 officers & men)

Vanguard Cavalry

Colonel & staff

Tver Dragoon Regiment (3 sqns. 200 officers & men)

Colonel & staff

Diatchkin Cossack Regiment (3 sotns. 200 officers & men)

Colonel & staff

Colonel & staff

2nd Kalmuck Regiment (3 sotns. 200 officers & men)

Pavlovgrad Hussar Regiment (8 sqns. 400 officers & men)

Colonel & staff

1st Bashkir Regiment (3 sotns. 200 officers & men)

Army of the Danube

Advance Guard

Commander:
Generalmajor
Count Lambert
& staff

Colonel & staff

1st Battalion, 14th Jäger Regiment
(360 officers & men)

2nd Battalion, 14th Jäger Regiment
(360 officers & men)

3rd Battalion, 14th Jäger Regiment
(360 officers & men)

Colonel & staff

1st Battalion, 27th Jäger Regiment
(360 officers & men)

3rd Battalion, 27th Jäger Regiment
(360 officers & men)

Colonel & staff

1st Battalion, 38th Jäger Regiment
(360 officers & men)

3rd Battalion, 38th Jäger Regiment
(360 officers & men)

Transport & Supply

Company, Equipment Train

Medical Service

Ambulance Company

Army of the Danube

Advance Guard

Artillery

Colonel & staff

Starodoub Dragoon Regiment (4 sqns. 240 officers & men)

Colonel & staff

Arasmass Dragoon Regiment (4 sqns. 240 officers & men)

11th Horse Battery (8 x 6 pdrs, 4 x 10 pdr Licornes, 216 officers & men)

Colonel & staff

Jitomir Dragoon Regiment (4 sqns. 240 officers & men)

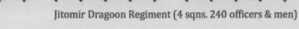

Colonel & staff

Alexandria Hussar Regiment (8 sqns. 400 officers & men)

Colonel & staff

Tartar Uhlan Regiment (8 sqns. 400 officers & men)

Army of the Danube

Advance Guard

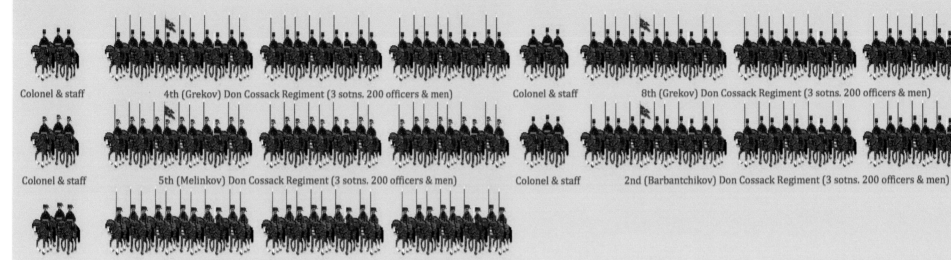

Colonel & staff

4th (Grekov) Don Cossack Regiment (3 sotns, 200 officers & men)

Colonel & staff

8th (Grekov) Don Cossack Regiment (3 sotns, 200 officers & men)

Colonel & staff

5th (Melinkov) Don Cossack Regiment (3 sotns, 200 officers & men)

Colonel & staff

2nd (Barbantchikov) Don Cossack Regiment (3 sotns, 200 officers & men)

Colonel & staff

Eupatorie Tartar Regiment (3 sotns, 200 officers & men)

Artillery

Colonel & staff

12th Horse Battery (8 x 6 pdrs, 4 x 10 pdr Licornes,
216 officers & men)

 **Transport & Supply**

Company, Equipment Train

 **Medical Service**

Ambulance Company

Commander:
General of
Infantry Langeron
& staff

22nd Infantry Division

Commander:
Generalmajor
& staff

Commander:
Generalmajor
& staff

1st Brigade

Transport, Supply & Medical Service

Colonel & staff

1st Battalion, Viborg Infantry Regiment
(360 officers & men)

3rd Battalion, Viborg Infantry Regiment
(360 officers & men)

Company, Equipment Train

Colonel & staff

1st Battalion, Vyatka Infantry Regiment
(360 officers & men)

3rd Battalion, Vyatka Infantry Regiment
(360 officers & men)

Ambulance Company

Artillery

Colonel & staff

22nd Position (Foot) Battery (8 x 12 pdrs, 4 x 20 pdr
unicorns, 233 officers & men)

Position (Foot) Battery (8 x 12 pdrs, 4 x 20 pdr
unicorns, 233 officers & men)

I Infantry Corps

Commander:
Generalmajor
& staff

22nd Infantry Division

Transport, Supply & Medical Service

2nd Brigade

Colonel & staff

1st Battalion, Stary Oskol Infantry Regiment
(360 officers & men)

3rd Battalion, Stary Oskol Infantry Regiment
(360 officers & men)

Company, Equipment Train

Colonel & staff

1st Battalion, 29th Jäger Regiment
(360 officers & men)

3rd Battalion, 29th Jäger Regiment
(360 officers & men)

Ambulance Company

Colonel & staff

1st Battalion, 45th Jäger Regiment
(360 officers & men)

Artillery

Light (Foot) Battery (6 x 6 pdrs, 6 x 10 pdr unicorns,
160 officers & men)

Light (Foot) Battery (6 x 6 pdrs, 6 x 10 pdr unicorns,
160 officers & men)

I Infantry Corps

Commander:
Generalmajor
& staff

Cavalry Brigade

Colonel & staff

Saint-Petersburg Dragoon Regiment (4 sqns. 240 officers & men)

Colonel & staff

Lifland Dragoon Regiment (4 sqns. 260 officers & men)

Colonel & staff

Panteleyev II Don Cossack Regiment (5 sotns. 320 officers & men)

Artillery

14th Horse Battery (8 x 6 pdrs, 4 x 10 pdr Licornes,
216 officers & men)

II Infantry Corps

Commander:
Generalmajor
Engelhard
& staff

8th Infantry Division

Commander:
Generalmajor
& staff

Commander:
Generalmajor
& staff

Transport, Supply & Medical Service

1st Brigade

Colonel & staff

1st Battalion, Archangel Infantry Regiment
(360 officers & men)

3rd Battalion, Archangel Infantry Regiment
(360 officers & men)

Company, Equipment Train

Colonel & staff

1st Battalion, Schlüsselburg Infantry Regiment
(360 officers & men)

3rd Battalion, Schlüsselburg Infantry Regiment
(360 officers & men)

  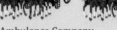 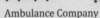

Ambulance Company

Colonel & staff

1st Battalion, 37th Jäger Regiment
(360 officers & men)

3rd Battalion, 37th Jäger Regiment
(360 officers & men)

II Infantry Corps

Commander:
Generalmajor
& staff

8th Infantry Division

2nd Brigade

Transport, Supply & Medical Service

Colonel & staff

1st Battalion, Old Ingermanland Infantry Regiment (360 officers & men)

3rd Battalion, Old Ingermanland Infantry Regiment (360 officers & men)

Company, Equipment Train

Colonel & staff

1st Battalion, Ukraine Infantry Regiment (360 officers & men)

3rd Battalion, Ukraine Infantry Regiment (360 officers & men)

Ambulance Company

Artillery

Colonel & staff

39th Position (Foot) Battery (8 x 12 pdrs, 4 x 20 pdr unicorns, 233 officers & men)

Light (Foot) Battery (6 x 6 pdrs, 6 x 10 pdr unicorns, 160 officers & men)

II Infantry Corps

Commander:
Generalmajor
& staff

Cavalry Brigade

Colonel & staff

Sievers Dragoon Regiment (4 sqns. 240 officers & men)

Colonel & staff

Smolensk Dragoon Regiment (4 sqns. 240 officers & men)

Artillery

15th Horse Battery (8 x 6 pdrs, 4 x 10 pdr Licornes,
216 officers & men)

III Infantry Corps

Commander:
Generalleutnant
Alexander
Voinov & staff

10th Infantry Division

Commander:
Generalleutnant
Lieven & staff

Commander:
Generalmajor
& staff

1st Brigade

Transport, Supply & Medical Service

Colonel & staff

1st Battalion, Kursk Infantry Regiment
(360 officers & men)

3rd Battalion, Kursk Infantry Regiment
(360 officers & men)

Company, Equipment Train

Colonel & staff

1st Battalion, Crimea Infantry Regiment
(360 officers & men)

3rd Battalion, Crimea Infantry Regiment
(360 officers & men)

Ambulance Company

Artillery

Colonel & staff

10th Position (Foot) Battery (8 x 12 pdrs, 4 x 20
pdr unicorns, 233 officers & men)

III Infantry Corps

Commander:
Generalmajor
& staff

10th Infantry Division

2nd Brigade

Transport, Supply & Medical Service

Colonel & staff

1st Battalion, Bialystok Infantry Regiment
(360 officers & men)

3rd Battalion, Bialystok Infantry Regiment
(360 officers & men)

Company, Equipment Train

Colonel & staff

1st Battalion, 8th Jäger Regiment
(360 officers & men)

3rd Battalion, 8th Jäger Regiment
(360 officers & men)

Ambulance Company

Colonel & staff

1st Battalion, 39th Jäger Regiment
(360 officers & men)

3rd Battalion, 39th Jäger Regiment
(360 officers & men)

Artillery

Pioneers

38th Light (Foot) Battery (6 x 6 pdrs, 6 x 10 pdr
unicorns, 160 officers & men)

50th Light (Foot) Battery (6 x 6 pdrs, 6 x 10 pdr
unicorns, 160 officers & men)

Pioneer Battalion & Equipment Train Coy.
(300 officers & men)

III Infantry Corps

Commander:
Generalleutnant
Sabaniev & staff

Provisional Infantry Division

Commander:
Generalmajor
& staff

1st Brigade

Artillery

Colonel & staff

1st Battalion, Olonetsk Infantry Regiment
(360 officers & men)

3rd Battalion, Olonetsk Infantry Regiment
(360 officers & men)

Colonel & staff

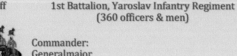

1st Battalion, Yaroslav Infantry Regiment
(360 officers & men)

3rd Battalion, Yaroslav Infantry Regiment
(360 officers & men)

Position (Foot) Battery (8 x 12 pdrs, 4 x 20 pdr
unicorns, 233 officers & men)

Commander:
Generalmajor
& staff

2nd Brigade

Colonel & staff

1st Battalion, Galicia Infantry Regiment
(360 officers & men)

3rd Battalion, Galicia Infantry Regiment
(360 officers & men)

Colonel & staff

1st Battalion, 12th Jäger Regiment
(360 officers & men)

Colonel & staff

1st Battalion, 7th Jäger Regiment
(360 officers & men)

3rd Battalion, 7th Jäger Regiment
(360 officers & men)

3rd Battalion, 12th Jäger Regiment
(360 officers & men)

III Infantry Corps

Commander:
Generalmajor
& staff

Cavalry Brigade

Colonel & staff

Kinbourn Dragoon Regiment (4 sqns. 260 officers & men)

Colonel & staff

Belarussian Hussar Regiment (8 sqns. 420 officers & men)

Colonel & staff

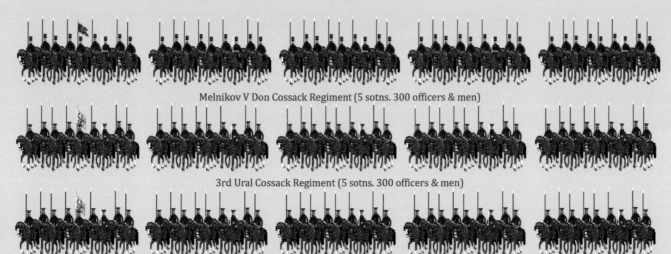

Melnikov V Don Cossack Regiment (5 sotns. 300 officers & men)

Colonel & staff

3rd Ural Cossack Regiment (5 sotns. 300 officers & men)

Colonel & staff

4th Ural Cossack Regiment (5 sotns. 300 officers & men)

Commander:
Generalmajor
Bulatov & staff

16th Infantry Division

Commander:
Generalmajor
& staff

Commander:
Generalmajor
& staff

2nd Brigade

Colonel & staff

1st Battalion, Nyslott Infantry Regiment
(380 officers & men)

3rd Battalion, Nyslott Infantry Regiment
(380 officers & men)

Colonel & staff

1st Battalion, Okhotsk Infantry Regiment
(360 officers & men)

Colonel & staff

1st Battalion, Kamchatka Infantry Regiment
(360 officers & men)

3rd Battalion, Kamchatka Infantry Regiment
(360 officers & men)

3rd Battalion, Okhotsk Infantry Regiment
(360 officers & men)

Artillery

Colonel & staff

16th Position (Foot) Battery (8 x 12 pdrs, 4 x 20
pdr unicorns, 233 officers & men)

Position (Foot) Battery (8 x 12 pdrs, 4 x 20 pdr
unicorns, 233 officers & men)

Position (Foot) Battery (8 x 12 pdrs, 4 x 20 pdr
unicorns, 233 officers & men)

Transport & Supply

Company, Equipment Train

Medical Service

Ambulance Company

IV Infantry Corps

Commander:
Generalmajor
& staff

Cavalry Brigade

Colonel & staff

Pereyaslavl Dragoon Regiment, (4 sqns. 240 officers & men)

Colonel & staff

Tirapol Dragoon Regiment, (4 sqns. 240 officers & men)

Colonel & staff

Chuguyev Uhlan Regiment (6 sqns. 380 officers & men)

Colonel & staff

Melnikov III Don Cossack Regiment (5 sotns. 300 officers & men)

Colonel & staff

Kuteynikov IV Don Cossack Regiment (5 sotns. 300 officers & men)

Reserve Corps

Commander:
Generalmajor
Ertel & staff

Commander:
Colonel & staff

1st Brigade

Transport, Supply & Medical Service

Major & staff

1st Combined Grenadier Battalion, 25th
Reserve Division (405 officers & men)

2nd Combined Grenadier Battalion, 25th
Reserve Division (405 officers & men)

Company, Equipment Train

Major & staff

1st Combined Battalion, 36th Reserve Division
(405 officers & men)

2nd Combined Battalion, 36th Reserve Division
(405 officers & men)

Ambulance Company

Major & staff

1st Combined Battalion, 37th Reserve Division
(405 officers & men)

2nd Combined Battalion, 37th Reserve Division
(405 officers & men)

Reserve Corps

Commander:
Colonel & staff

2nd Brigade

Transport, Supply & Medical Service

Major & staff

1st Combined Btn. 1st Regiment, 19th Reserve
Division (405 officers & men)

2nd Combined Btn. 1st Regiment, 19th Reserve
Division (405 officers & men)

Company, Equipment Train

Major & staff

1st Combined Btn. 2nd Regiment, 19th Reserve
Division (405 officers & men)

2nd Combined Btn. 2nd Regiment, 19th Reserve
Division (405 officers & men)

Ambulance Company

Major & staff

1st Combined Btn. 3rd Regiment, 19th Reserve
Division (405 officers & men)

2nd Combined Btn. 3rd Regiment, 19th Reserve
Division (405 officers & men)

Reserve Corps

Commander:
Colonel & staff

3rd Brigade

Transport, Supply & Medical Service

Major & staff

1st Combined Btn. 4th Regiment, 19th Reserve
Division (405 officers & men)

2nd Combined Btn. 4th Regiment, 19th Reserve
Division (405 officers & men)

Company, Equipment Train

Colonel & staff

1st Battalion, 16th Jäger Regiment
(405 officers & men)

3rd Battalion, 16th Jäger Regiment
(405 officers & men)

Ambulance Company

Colonel & staff

1st Battalion, 17th Jäger Regiment
(405 officers & men)

3rd Battalion, 17th Jäger Regiment
(405 officers & men)

Reserve Corps

Commander:
Colonel & staff

4th Brigade

Transport, Supply & Medical Service

Major & staff

1st Combined Btn. 1st Regiment, 20th Reserve Division (400 officers & men)

2nd Combined Btn. 1st Regiment, 20th Reserve Division (400 officers & men)

Company, Equipment Train

Major & staff

1st Combined Btn. 2nd Regiment, 20th Reserve Division (400 officers & men)

2nd Combined Btn. 2nd Regiment, 20th Reserve Division (400 officers & men)

Ambulance Company

Major & staff

1st Combined Btn. 3rd Regiment, 20th Reserve Division (400 officers & men)

2nd Combined Btn. 3rd Regiment, 20th Reserve Division (400 officers & men)

Reserve Corps

Commander:
Colonel & staff

5th Brigade

Transport, Supply & Medical Service

Major & staff

1st Combined Btn. 4th Regiment, 20th Reserve Division (400 officers & men)

2nd Combined Btn. 4th Regiment, 20th Reserve Division (400 officers & men)

Company, Equipment Train

Major & staff

1st Combined Btn. 5th Regiment, 20th Reserve Division (400 officers & men)

2nd Combined Btn. 5th Regiment, 20th Reserve Division (400 officers & men)

Ambulance Company

Colonel & staff

1st Battalion, 9th Jäger Regiment (400 officers & men)

3rd Battalion, 9th Jäger Regiment (400 officers & men)

Commander:
Colonel & staff

6th Brigade

Colonel & staff

1st Battalion, 15th Jäger Regiment (400 officers & men)

3rd Battalion, 15th Jäger Regiment (400 officers & men)

Colonel & staff

1st Battalion, 46th Jäger Regiment (400 officers & men)

3rd Battalion, 46th Jäger Regiment (400 officers & men)

Reserve Corps

 Commander: Generalmajor & staff

Cavalry Brigade

Major & staff — 1st Combined Dragoon Regiment, 2nd Reserve Cavalry Division (3 sqns. 300 offivers & men)

Major & staff — 2nd Combined Dragoon Regiment, 2nd Reserve Cavalry Division (3 sqns. 300 offivers & men)

Major & staff — 1st Combined Dragoon Regiment, 20th Reserve Cavalry Division (3 sqns. 300 offivers & men)

Major & staff — 2nd Combined Dragoon Regiment, 20th Reserve Cavalry Division (3 sqns. 300 offivers & men)

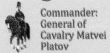 Commander:
General of
Cavalry Matvei
Platov

 ADCs to
General of
Cavalry Matvei
Platov

 Chief of Staff:
Generalmajor
& staff

 Commander:
Lt.Col. Maxim
Vlasov III
& staff

1st Brigade

 Lt.Col. Ivan
Andrianov II

 Host starshina
Mikhail
Chernozubov VIII

 Yesaul Stepan
Andronov III
& staff

 Lt.Col. Prince
Ahmed-bey
Khunkalov I
& staff

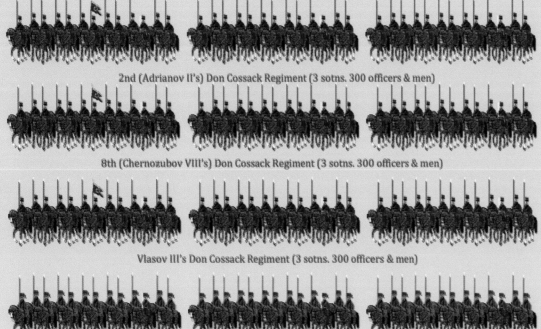

2nd (Adrianov II's) Don Cossack Regiment (3 sotns. 300 officers & men)

8th (Chernozubov VIII's) Don Cossack Regiment (3 sotns. 300 officers & men)

Vlasov III's Don Cossack Regiment (3 sotns. 300 officers & men)

Perekop Horse Tatar Regiment (3 sotns. 300 officers & men)

Cossack Corps

Commander:
Generalmajor
Nikolay Ilovaisky V
& staff

2nd Brigade

Host starshina
Ivan Davydov III

8th (Ilovaisyk) Don Cossack Regiment (3 sotns. 300 officers & men)

Host starshina
Alexey Grekov
& staff

18th (Grekov XVIII's) Don Cossack Regiment (3 sotns. 300 officers & men)

Commander:
Generalmajor
Vasily Denisov VII
& staff

3rd Brigade

Host starshina
Grigory Pobednov

Host starshina
Ivan Zhirov & staff

7th (Denisov VII's) Don Cossack Regiment (3 sotns. 300 officers & men)

Zhirov's Don Cossack Regiment (3 sotns. 300 officers & men)

Cossack Corps

Commander:
Generalmajor
Dmitri Kuteinikov
II & staff

5th Brigade

Lt.Col. Konstantin
Kharitonov VII

Lt.Col. Prince
Kaya-bey
Balatukov I & staff

Kharitonov VII's Don Cossack Regiment (3 sotns. 300 officers & men)

Simpferopolsk Horse Tartar Regiment (3 sotns. 300 officers & men)

Artillery

Host starshina
Peter Suvorov II
& staff

2nd Don Cossack Horse Artillery Battery (8 x 6 pdrs, 4 x 10 pdr
Licornes, 156 officers & men)

III Cavalry Corps

Commander:
Generallieutenant
Count Pahlen III

ADCs to
Generallieutenant
Count Pahlen III

Chief of Staff:
Generalmajor
& staff

Commander:
Generalmajor
Stepan Dyatkov
& staff

1st Brigade

Colonel Sergey
Ushakov & staff

Kourland Dragoon Regiment (4 sqns. 400 officers & men)

Lt.Col. Fedor
Zonnenbach
& staff

Orenburg Dragoon Regiment (4 sqns. 400 officers & men)

Commander:
Colonel Baron
Cyprian Creitz
& staff

2nd Brigade

Lt.Col. Anton
Yuzhakov & staff

Siberia Dragoon Regiment (4 sqns. 400 officers & men)

Major & staff

Irkurtsk Dragoon Regiment (4 sqns. 400 officers & men)

III Cavalry Corps

Commander:
Generalmajor Ivan
Dorokhov & staff

3rd Brigade

Colonel Prince
Ivan Vadbolsky
& staff

Mariupol Hussar Regiment (6 sqns. 560 officers & men)

Colonel David
Delyanov & staff

Soum Hussar Regiment (6 sqns. 560 officers & men)

Colonel Aleksey
Nikitin & staff

Artillery

1st Horse Battery (6 x 6 pdrs, 6 x 10 pdr unicorns,
160 officers & men)

3rd Horse Battery (6 x 6 pdrs, 6 x 10 pdr unicorns,
160 officers & men)

The Campaign and Battle

The Russian Campaign of 1812

The Russian campaign had opened with *La Grande Armée's* crossing of the river Nieman on 24th June 1812 and over the next few weeks, some 612,000 men from all over the empire would be committed to the invasion of Russia. This enormous multi-national army had been drawn together over the past year and represented the final solution to the deteriorated relations between the French and Russian empires. With a main army of about 450,000 men, Napoleon sought to bring the 200,000 men of the main Russian Western armies to a decisive battle that would end the campaign close to the border. Instead, the Russians commanded by General Barclay de Tolly, were loath to accept battle on such unequal terms and instead withdrew into Russia – laying waste to anything that would be useful to the enemy as they fell back.

The Russian withdrawal continued throughout the stifling summer heat of July while Napoleon and the central group of *La Grande Armée* numbering 250,000 men trudged on behind, steadily dwindling in numbers as they followed the Minsk to Vitebsk road. A number of battles and skirmished were fought over the coming weeks, but the predominant Russian strategy was one of withdrawal and 'scorched earth policy'. The toll this took on Napoleon's central army group was plain to see – by the time the first major battle took place at Smolensk on 16-18th August, the central group was down to about 185,000 men. A hollow victory at Smolensk led to another march eastwards as the Russians withdrew towards Moscow. By now Napoleon had accepted that his strategy to trap the Russian armies in the west of the country had failed. Instead he opted for an all-out advance on Moscow, despite the logistical challenges that caused and also against his senior commanders' advice.

Above: (1) Italian troops of IV Corps advancing into Russia during the summer of 1812 (2) One of the early clashes at Mir on 9-10th July between Russian cossacks and Polish uhlans of the Grand Duchy of Warsaw.

Above: The battle of Smolensk, 16-18th August 1812

the emperor finally accepted that peace would not come in Moscow and ordered a retreat to begin on 19th October.

Waiting in Moscow during the deceptively mild weather for so long had been a mistake. However, the withdrawal could be successful if enough supplies were available. So the route westwards was to follow a more southern route back to Smolensk via Kaluga so as to avoid the devastated countryside crossed during the advance. This plan was thwarted at Maloyaroslavets on 24th October when Kutuzov drove back part of Napoleon's army and blocked the route intended for the retreat. Rather than barrel through Kutuzov's army, Napoleon moved north west and continued along the Smolensk road that had been used during the advance. With little forage or supplies to be had, *La Grande Armée* was doomed to starvation. To add to this impending misery, the first snow fell on 4th November.

For their part, the Russians could not give up Moscow without a fight and the new commander, Prince Mikhail Kutuzov decided to give battle on 7th September at Borodino, 75 miles from Russia's second capital. The battle involved 130,000 Imperial troops and 120,000 Russians and was one of the most brutal battles in a period characterised by brutal battles. Some 70,000 casualties were inflicted during an unimaginative battle consisting mainly of frontal attacks that lasted for about twelve hours. This 'slogging match' punctuated by the fire of 1,200 cannon, would go down as the most costly single day's fighting of the Napoleonic Wars and the casualty rate would rarely be seen again until the Great War.

With victory gained – albeit a *'pyric'* one – The 108,000 survivors of *La Grande Armée's* central group entered Moscow on 14th September. Expecting the Russian's to accept peace now that he was in possession of the city, Napoleon waited in vain for five weeks for a response from the Czar. With fire having destroyed much of the city and supplies, and with nearby Russian forces growing stronger and more daring by the day,

Above: The battle of Borodino, 7th September 1812

The retreat continued and the French steadily lost men to hunger, cold weather and cossacks. Partisans had also been called to arms and isolated Imperial troops were being killed or captured in their hundreds. The supply train practically broke down as more and more horses succumbed to the bad weather and lack of forage. The cavalry practically ceased to exist and now numbered just a few thousand. Many of the dismounted horsemen either picked up a musket and joined the remaining organised infantry units, or just added their number to the growing throng of stragglers who fell out of the ranks at an alarming rate. Guns were abandoned en masse as draught animal died in droves. Regiments dwindled to such an extent that the survivors had to be merged with other regiments to form battalion sized units, themselves representing a once strong division.

Ney commanded the rearguard and would perform heroics during the retreat, being cut off with heavy losses and only later being able to rejoin *La Grande Armée* by crossing the unreliable ice of the Dnieper river on 17th November. Napoleon would dub him *'the bravest of the brave'* for his seemingly miraculous fortitude in holding off the pursuing Russians and brining his 800 survivors back safely. His reappearance was also a much needed tonic for the suffering column making its painful journey west.

The Imperial Guard had famously been left out of the fighting at Borodino, it was now this formation that possessed the strongest and most disciplined units. By the middle of November, the corps of Davout, Ney, Eugène, Poniatowski and Junot were mere shadows of their former march out strengths – and all the time, Kutuzov at the head of the 1st and 2nd Western Armies followed on a parallel route to the south and at a respectful distance. Cossacks followed *La Grande Armée* more closely and along a snow covered road littered with the corpses of men and horses and abandoned

Above (1) Ney and the rearguard (2) French dragoons crossing the Borodino battlefield during the retreat from Moscow.

guns, weapons, equipment and wagons. Further Russian armies were closing in under Wittgenstein, Steinheil and Tchichagov intent on trapping *La Grande Armée* and preventing an escape across the river Berezina.

Kutuzov next moved to block Napoleon on 14th November and a series of skirmishes fought at Krasnoy over the next four days resulted in 26,000 Imperial losses in killed, wounded or captured (mostly stragglers) to a Russian loss of around 5,000. Napoleon was however, able to push through and continue the retreat.

As the army continued past Smolensk and Vitebsk, supplies and reinforcements became the uppermost priority. Russian troops had moved and captured the supply magazine at Polotsk the month before, then captured another one at Vitebsk. The one at Minsk still remained intact – for the time being. The army had by now dwindled to just 20,000 men but would soon be joined at the river Bobr by 30,000 reinforcements under Victor, Oudinot and Dombrowski during the third week of November. The now 50,000 strong army with about 40,000 stragglers continued the retreat towards the proposed crossing at the river Berezina which was frozen and was expected to facilitate a crossing on foot.

The capture of Minsk, 17th November 1812

A garrison of 2,000 infantry under the command of *Général de brigade* Bronikowski had been placed inside Minsk to defend the city and protect valuable supplies stored there. The force was composed of two battalions of the 22nd Lithuanian Infantry Regiment assisted by a French *bataillon de marche* that had recently stopped there en route. Minsk held two million rations which were vitally important to *La Grande Armée* at this stage in the campaign. There were also about 2,000 wounded housed in the city and 110 Russian prisoners held there.

Above (1) Napoleon during the retreat amidst the infantry of the Guard
(2) The battle of Krasnoy 15-18th November 1812,

The Advance Guard of Admiral Tchichagov's Army of the Danube had advanced on Minsk under the command of *Generalmajor* Count Lambert. This force of 3,600 men and 36 guns was in place outside the city by 17th November. Offering some initial resistance, Bronikowski was obliged to abandon the city and attempt to bring his command to the main army, but around 2,000 men (including wounded) were captured on the Vilnius road at Rakov.

The loss of the supplies at Minsk was a serious blow for *La Grande Armée* and more bad news was too follow. As Napoleon's remaining troops neared the Berezina river, a sudden thaw caused the frozen surface to melt and the river became a flowing torrent of released ice. A suitable crossing place had however, been identified at Borisov and a force of 5,000 men (mostly the fresh Polish 17th Division) under *Général de division* Dombrowski was sent to secure it.

The first clash at Borisov, 21st November 1812

Generalmajor Count Lambert at the head of the 4,500 strong Advance Guard of the Army of the Danube, had continued their march to the Berezina following their success at Minsk. They now fell upon Dombrowski's garrison at Borisov intent on taking the bridge there. The Polish troops offered stiff resistance, but the Russians were determined to capture the river crossing and prevent *La Grande Armée's* escape. Heavy losses (about 2,000 men) were sustained by the seven jaeger battalions and the two battalions of the Vitebsk infantry regiment before the Poles began to waver. The Russians were then able to capture most of the Imperial troops except for supporting Guard cavalry and the 1st Polish Infantry Regiment.

On 23rd November, an attempt was made to retake Borisov but Lambert simply destroyed the bridge and remained on the west bank of the Berezina while Russian reinforcements approached from various directions – Wittgenstein and 30,000 men shadowing Napoleon from the north, Chichagov with 35,000 coming from Minsk to the west and Miloradovich with 32,000 following *La Grande Armée* from the east. Kutuzov was also in the vicinity with a further 39,000 men but would be too far off (40 miles to the east) to intervene.

Above: (1) The combat at Baturi on 24th November 1812 (2) Russian Generalmajor Count Lambert, commander of the Advance Guard of the Army of the Danube.

Heavily outnumbered and short of cavalry, it was also on this day that Napoleon ordered all remaining officers who still possessed a horse to assemble at headquarters, where they were formed into a 600 man strong mounted ad-hoc imperial escort unit, termed *'L'escadron sacré'* (sacred squadron) and composed of 4 companies (each under a general) with *Général de division* Grouchy in overall command. Their orders were to stay close to imperial headquarters at all times.

The clash at Baturi, 24th November 1812

Wittgenstein's Advance Guard under *Generalmajor* Harpe caught up with Victor's rearguard at Baturi on 24th November. Harpe commanded about 4,000 men with 18 guns which he launched upon a similar number of imperial troops – Badeners and Bergisch troops of the 26th Division under *Général de division* Daendels. The result was another Russian victory but losses on both sides were light at a few hundred in total.

Above: Polish generals of V Corps (left) Général de brigade Kniaziewicz, commander of the 17th Division and (right) Général de division Krasinski, commander of the 18th Division. Below left: much of the army's heavy cavalry was lost or un-mounted by November and just three French cuirassier regiments were available

Napoleon's army continued to approach the Berezina and since the loss of the bridge at Borisov, all hopes now rested on a shallow stretch of the river that could facilitate a crossing place recently discovered by Polish cavalry. Located 8 miles north of Borisov at Studienka, it would however require the construction of trestle bridges across both the river and its muddy banks. This would be a challenge since the bridging train had been abandoned at Orcha. But since the pontoon train commander, *Général de division* Eblé had held onto a number of field forges, it would be possible to construct bridges from local materials. Surviving members of the army's sapper and pontoon companies from the various corps were ordered to join Eblé and *Général de division* Chasseloup-Laubat at Studienka and work began on the bridges on 25th November. Diversions were planned but the work would continue under the very noses of Chichagov's camps across the river at Brili.

The main diversion unfolded when *Maréchal* Oudinot and II Corps manoeuvred towards Borisov. Chichagov believed this signalled Napoleon's intention to attempt a crossing there or more likely further downstream. Initially leaving 3,000 men under *Generalmajor* Tchlapitz at Brili, the bulk of Chichagov's army march south of Borisov to Szabaszeviki intent on patrolling a 55 miles stretch of the river. The 3,000 men at Brili were then ordered to Borisov – leaving a possible crossing at Studienka uncontested. The following day and now fully aware that the camp at Brili had been abandoned, a unit of 40 French cavalry swam their horses across the river followed by 400 infantrymen in small boats to establish a forward defensive position to protect the French bridge builders while they completed their work. The river was up to 30 yards wide at this point but there was also about the same distance in marshy land at either bank that also needed to be bridged. Eblé set out to build two bridges (one for the infantry and cavalry, the other for the artillery) using timbers taken from the nearby villages and from Studienka itself.

Top: The building of the bridges.. Above (left) Général de division Eblé, in charge of the bridge building and (right) Général de division Doumerc, commanding 400 survivors of the 3rd Cuirassier Division. (left a modern view from Studienka during the winter.

Napoleon was watching patiently as the troops moved up to the river bank to make the crossing. He was observed by a Würtemberg soldier from III Corps who remembered:

"When we came nearer the Berezina River, there was a place where Napoleon ordered his pack horses to be unharnessed and where he ate. He watched his army pass by in the most wretched condition. What he may have felt in his heart is impossible to surmise. His outward appearance seemed indifferent and unconcerned over the wretchedness of his soldiers; only ambition and lost honour may have made themselves felt in his heart; and, although the French and Allies shouted into his ears many oaths and curses about his own guilty person, he was still able to listen to them unmoved."

With the bridges ready, Napoleon began moving his troops across – constantly fearing that the Russians would realise what was afoot. But it was not until the night of 26-27th November that Tchlapitz and his 3,000 men at Borisov became aware of the crossing and hastened back towards Brili when they were stopped by Oudinot's battalions. Beginning to realise his error and seeing no imperial troops downstream from Borisov, Chichagov ordered his army back but did not immediately move against Brili as his troops were still assembling.

Napoleon and the Guard were across the river by midday on 27th November and by late afternoon one of the bridges gave way again, requiring that the sappers and *pontonniers* wade out again to repair it for a third time. By nightfall, I and IV Corps had crossed while IX Corps under *Maréchal* Victor remained on the eastern bank to delay Wittgenstein's army which had just arrived at Borisov.

Right (1) The crossing of the Berezina river on 29th November 1812 (2) Modern view of the Berezina from the original site of the infantry and cavalry bridge.

The combat at Staroi-Borisov, 27th November 1812

One division of IX Corps formed the rearguard – the 12th under *Général de division* Partoneaux. This was a strong and fresh force numbering around 11,500 French and Dutch infantry with six guns and supported by just under 500 men of the Saxon Prinz Johann *Chevaulegers.*

Partoneaux received orders during the day to withdraw from Borisov and join the rest of II Corps at Studienka. However, it seems he delayed his march due to confusion in the ranks and vehicles blocking his route. Setting off that night, his division blundered into around 18,000 Russians from Wittgenstein's and Steinheil's corps. Outnumbered and called upon by Wittgenstein to surrender, Partoneaux replied *"I do not want to surrender, you shall witness the effort we're going to make to open up a way through for ourselves".* There followed a fierce series of bayonet charges and musketry fire as he and his men tried to force their way through to Studienka. Partoneaux next rode out with several officers to scout a possible escape route but the group were surprised and captured by a cossack patrol.

Without their commander and completely overwhelmed, the 12th Division were repulsed then held in place until being compelled to surrender the following morning. The 260 surviving troopers of the Saxon Prinz Johann *Chevaulegers,* tried to find their own way out but lost their way and also surrendered. Around 8,000 men were killed or captured – only the 4th battalion of the 55th *Infantry de ligne* from the provisional infantry regiment escaped along with 4 guns. It was here that Wittgenstein finally linked up with Chichagov to co-ordinate their efforts against Napoleon's army on both banks of the Berezina.

Right: (1) French 12th Division try to fight their way out at Staroi-Borisov on 27th November (2) A late 19th century painting of Studienka near the site of the bridges.

The battle of the Berezina, 28-29th November 1812

Later on the morning of the 28th November, part of Chichagov's Army of the Danube spearheaded by *Generalmajor* Tchlapitz and the Vanguard, attacked Oudinot's forward most battalions on the west bank of the Berezina and slowly pushed them back towards Brili. Oudinot fell wounded and command in this sector fell to *Maréchal* Ney who led the Swiss and Dutch troops of the 9th Division in several daring bayonet charges. As Chichagov's army closed in with the French, a series of fire fights involving 25,000 men began that would last until nightfall until *Général de division* Doumerc at the head of the 400 survivors of the 3rd Cuirassier Division, made a charge that drove the Russians back and ended the fighting on the west bank for that day.

Since 5:00 am that same morning, Wittgenstein had been attacking *Maréchal* Victor and IX Corps on the eastern bank of the river. The Berg and Baden troops distinguished themselves by their fierce resistance but were gradually pushed back with heavy loss after 8 hours of fighting. At one point, the remaining Baden hussars and Hessian Garde *Chevaulegers,* about 350 men under *General de brigade* Fournier-Sarlovèze, made a heroic but suicidal charge against superior numbers from which just 50 men returned.

Since 1:00 pm Russian guns had been sighted on high ground that allowed them to fire with impunity onto the bridges and also on the troops on the east bank – although most of their shots fell amongst the vast horde of stragglers who were driven into a stampede for the river crossings. When the cannonade stopped four hours later, the bridge builders set to work clearing a path so Victor's IX Corps could cross over to the western bank.

Right: (1) The final stages of the river crossings on 29th November (2) Dutch infantry from the French 9th Division of Oudinot's Corps, stubbornly protect the river crossings.

It was 10:00 pm when the remains of IX Corps actually crossed the river to safety, and with the bridges now free of combat troops, an opportunity presented itself to the 40,000 stragglers to cross. But despite calls to do so, they stayed put on the eastern bank and lit their campfires for the night. That night, Napoleon issued orders to Eblé to burn the bridges at 7:00 am the next morning. Eblé however, delayed executing the order until 8:30 am in the hope that some of the stragglers would cross. Despite the delay, most stayed put and only raised themselves when the realisation that they were being abandoned dawned on them. Sergeant Bourgogne of the Guard Fusiliers tells us what happened next:

"The unfortunate men who had not taken advantage of the night to get away had at the first appearance of dawn rushed on to the bridge, but now it was too late. Preparations were already made to burn it down. Numbers jumped into the water, hoping to swim through the floating bits of ice, but not one reached the shore. I saw them all there in water up to their shoulders, and, overcome by the terrible cold, they all miserably perished. On the bridge was a canteen man carrying a child on his head. His wife was in front of him, crying bitterly. I could not stay any longer, it was more than I could bear. Just as I turned away, a cart containing a wounded officer fell from the bridge, with the horse also. They next set fire to the bridge, and I have been told that scenes impossible to describe for horror then took place."

Left: Troops of La Grande Armée safely across the Berezina. Above right, French troops helping the well-known surgeon of the Imperial Guard, Baron Larrey to cross the bridge.

With both bridges now in flames, the cossacks and troops from Wittgenstein's army, swept down on those unfortunates remaining on the eastern bank with their numerous baggage waggons. Those who would not brave the icy waters of the Berezina were taken prisoner or put out of their misery. *Generalmajor* Yermalov of the Russian artillery tells us that....

"Near the bridges, which were partially destroyed, guns and transport wagons had fallen into the river. Crowds of people, including many women, children and infants, had moved down to the ice-covered river. Nobody could escape from the terrible frost. No one could ever witness a more terrible sight. ... The river was covered with ice which was as transparent as glass: there were many dead bodies visible beneath it across the whole width of the river. The enemy had abandoned huge numbers of guns and wagons. The treasures of ransacked Moscow had also not succeeded in getting across the river."

The well-known painting by Polish artist January Suchodolski depicting La Grande Armée Crossing the Berezina

With no means of crossing the river, Wittgenstein remained on the eastern bank while Napoleon and the remnants of *La Grande Armée* continued their retreat towards Vilnius. Chichagov gave orders for a pursuit but this would be hampered when the French destroyed the bridges through the Gaina swamp between Brili and the Zembin road that led to the Lithuanian capital. The battle of the Berezina was over and a tactical victory had been gained by Napoleon. In part, this was due to poor co-ordination and failure to press home the attack on the part of the Russians. But also due to the heroic performance of the remaining disciplined units and the bridge builders who had facilitated their escape.

The further losses inflicted on the already much weakened *Grande Armée,* had been enormous: around 22,000 combatants had fallen or been taken captive, along with about 25,000 stragglers captured - most of whom (including women and children) would succumb to starvation or the cold. II and IX Corps had both been reduced by about half following their selfless efforts to protect the crossing. But of the 250 or so guns still with *La Grande Armée* at the Berezina, it appears that just 25 were lost.

Some 40,000 men and much of the remaining baggage had survived to continue the retreat westwards. The Russian casualties were probably around 25,000 in total of killed and wounded. The retreat would continue into December and follow the road via Molodechno and Smorgoni until Vilnius was reached, but there would be no further military confrontations as the Russian armies held back and allowed the plummeting temperatures and the cossacks to finish their work. Of course, the Russians were also suffering considerable loss to the cold but were at least provisioned to bear the worst of it.

Left: (1) After the Berezina the retreat continued as the temperatures dropped further (2) the surviving soldiers of La Grande Armée reached the Lithuanian capital of Vilnius on 9th December 1812

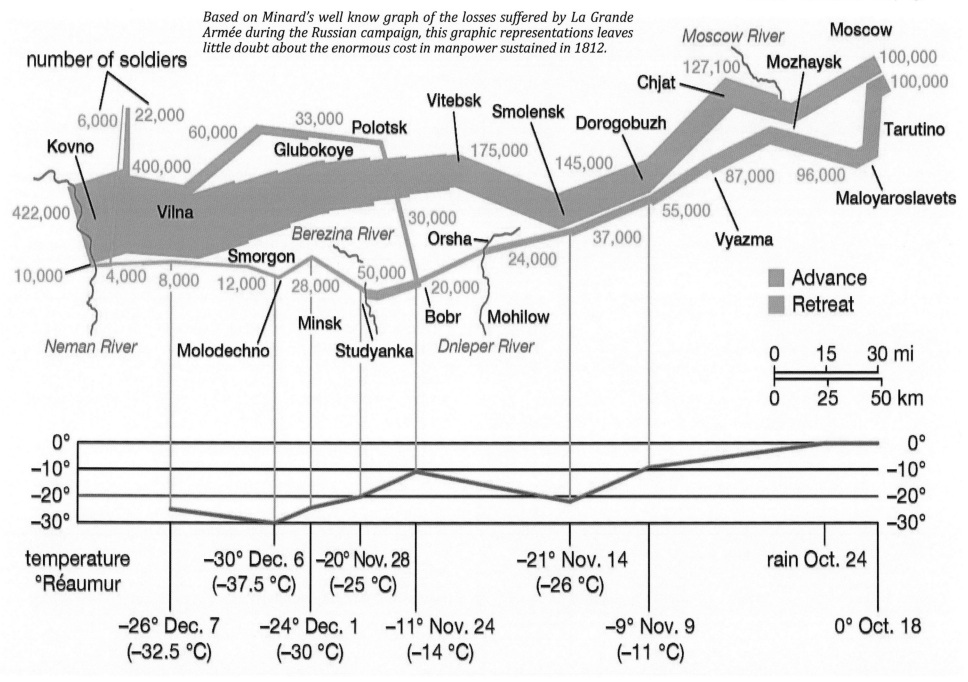

Based on Minard's well know graph of the losses suffered by La Grande Armée during the Russian campaign, this graphic representations leaves little doubt about the enormous cost in manpower sustained in 1812.

number of soldiers

Moscow River
Moscow
127,100
Mozhaysk
100,000
Chjat
100,000
Vitebsk
Smolensk
Dorogobuzh
Tarutino
22,000
6,000
33,000
Polotsk
175,000
145,000
60,000
Glubokoye
Kovno
400,000
87,000
96,000
422,000
Vilna
Maloyaroslavets
30,000
Orsha
55,000
10,000
4,000
8,000
12,000
28,000
50,000
Berezina River
24,000
Vyazma
37,000
Smorgon
20,000
Neman River
Minsk
Bobr
Mohilow
Advance
Molodechno
Studyanka
Dnieper River
Retreat

0   15   30 mi
0   25   50 km

temperature
°Réaumur

–30° Dec. 6
(–37.5 °C)

–20° Nov. 28
(–25 °C)

–21° Nov. 14
(–26 °C)

rain Oct. 24

–26° Dec. 7
(–32.5 °C)

–24° Dec. 1
(–30 °C)

–11° Nov. 24
(–14 °C)

–9° Nov. 9
(–11 °C)

0° Oct. 18

The weather got even colder after the Berezina and by the first week of December dropped to -26c then -30c. As starvation broke down all remaining discipline (except for the Guard) the 40,000 that escaped at the Berezina were down to about 25,000 by 1st December. On 5th December and at the insistence of his senior commanders, Napoleon abandoned the army at Smorgoni to return post-haste to Paris by sleigh. Travelling incognito across Europe with a small cavalry escort, he reached the capital on the night of 17th December. Command of the army passed to Murat who continued on to Vilnius with about 14,000 formed troops and tens of thousands of stragglers. The Lithuanian capital was reached on 9th December but just 8,000 men plus the stragglers remained. The Nieman was re-crossed on 14th December and Murat left the army in the hands of Prince Eugène who brought the pitiful remnants back into Germany via Kovno. Just around 10,000 made it to Königsberg and that was counting further reinforcements added recently on the way.

Over the next few weeks detached forces started to regroup including Schwarzenberg's Austrians and Reynier's Saxons. Around 112,000 are thought to have left Russia from the 612,000 committed. However, many of the survivors were broken down and suffering from frostbite. The Russians had also suffered heavily and only a third of the force that had marched from Maloyaroslavets remained when Vilnius was reached.

The enormous casualties suffered by *La Grande Armée* in the campaign can be broken down as follows – 100, 000 died in action, 200,000 died from disease or starvation, 50,000 were abandoned in hospitals, 50,000 deserted and 100,000 became prisoners of war. The Russian losses were closely comparable and estimated at 200,000 killed, 50,000 missing or deserted and 150,000 wounded. Counting civilian deaths from starvation caused by the burning of crops or looting their supplies, well over a million people overall are estimated to have died.

The blow to the Napoleonic military capability cannot be understated. In addition to the massive loss in manpower, a thousand guns were lost along with most of the cavalry and draught horses that had been taken into Russia. Napoleon would rebuild his army and fight a new campaign in the spring of 1813, this time facing Prussians as well as Russians. *La Grande Armée* though, to all intent and purpose, had largely been lost in Russia, and neither the soldiers replacing it nor the new horses procured for the cavalry and artillery, would be able to prevent the looming defeat. By October 1813 and facing a combined Europe that included former allies Prussia, Austria and Bavaria, that defeat would be driven home in Saxony and soon most German states would also join the alliance against France. This new war would then sweep into France itself during the first months of 1814, eventually leading to Napoleon's inevitable abdication and exile. As a final chapter in the Napoleonic story, that exile would briefly be interrupted by a new war in 1815 ending in final defeat at Waterloo.

Other books in this series

All books available on Amazon in kindle and print format.

Future titles at planning/research stage include:

Aspern-Essling, the armies of 1809

Austrian Campaign, the other battles of 1809

Printed in Great Britain
by Amazon